Leadership:

An Incumbent of Faith

Dr. Moses Haregewoyn

Dr. Moses Haregewoyn

Leadership: An Incumbent of Faith

Table of Contents

Dr. Moses Haregewoyn

Leadership: An Incumbent of Faith

Blank Page Left Intentionally

Dr. Moses Haregewoyn

Introduction

In my view, every religion, whether it is Buddhism, Islam, or Christianity, teaches humankind some values and principles essential to life. To respect other people, not cause harm to anyone, and live in peace and harmony with your loved ones and community are some of the few and most basic ethics and morals laid down by all kinds of religions. Peace and harmony lie at the core of every religion.

When one follows their religion, in essence, they follow a set of rules. That, in turn, gives birth to another discipline. We all have goals set by our respective religions that we must accomplish and that we have to work towards.

For example, if someone's goal is to please their God, their maker, then they will stay determined and resolute on their path to a religious commitment to their God and not rest until they have accomplished their goal. That contributes to a person's ability to become a good team player and a leader side by side.

This is what I would like to show to my readers. I have become successful, and I believe that is so because of my faith. I worked hard and still continue to do so. This is the calling that led me here. I want to do good things. I want to help people who need help the most. In the past, when I had made a commitment with myself and my God to help others, I would fulfill that commitment by using the means that my God provided me to mentor people and to give to the community - to the employees. Not only was I coming to the aid of other people, but also serving God simultaneously.

When you decide to search for the truth - the truth being the acknowledgment of the existence of God and your unwavering belief in him - you automatically start clinging to hope and avoid engaging in any activities that may incur you the wrath or anger of your Lord.

The same principle applies when you want to excel in the worldly domains of life. In order to make any venture successful, you must believe in yourself and your God to safely walk you to your destination.

All the deities that people look up to and worship as their Gods, be it Jesus or Buddha or the various other religious leaders, are all valid examples of doing what they preach. They all lived their lives with the utmost honesty, integrity, and fear of God. They have lived exemplary lives. That's

Leadership: An Incumbent of Faith

what I'm trying to show through this book. Leadership through faith. This book will not only teach you how to become a better leader regarding your worldly affairs, say family, friends, and guiding your community, but also how to become a successful leader in the eyes of God.

I also want to mention the role of leadership in working organizations today. Our workplaces play an integral role in our life by giving us a set schedule, discipline, and a sense of community and helping us rise up the ladder. This cannot be done without the help of effective leadership. The managers and supervisors running the show can either bring the best out of us or let us remain the same. This is why enlightened leadership is integral in the workplace.

The kind of people who lead us can inspire in ways we ourselves do not know, but it is important for them to have a vision and sense of direction for others to follow. They need to set an example of how one should behave at the office. This aspect will be heavily explored in the book.

We have an eye-opening example in the situation of the Covid-19 pandemic experienced in the past two years. It was a game-changer for many of us around the world. It affected us without caring for our wealth or anything else for that matter. It was a cruel reminder from God that we must solidify as one community, as one people, regardless of what race or religion we belong to, and help see the innumerable reasons that bind us all together instead of the few numbered differences that we tend to highlight.

It was also the first time in the history of the world wherein people turned to each other for help, and our leaders really did show us the way out of the horrendous situation into which the pandemic had plunged us all. When many of us lost our loved ones and endured immeasurable loss, strangers turned up at our doors to pay their respects and join us in our bereavement.

The world was given a reality check, and many things that were deemed impossible were proven to be probable with the advent of the virus. People were allowed to work from their homes which changed the working dynamics completely. This happened because those who called themselves our 'leaders' finally decided to exude leadership qualities.

This even brought a tremendous change in how we work, where we work, and why it can be made better. Technology played a considerable role in keeping the world together and getting work done. It even changed the usual dynamics of working at the office to working from home. This trend has stayed consistent even after the end of the lockdown, and many wonder what else is in store. Yet, in those times, we saw businesses either fall apart or rise in the hard times. This highlights how leaders did their part for better or for worse.

Through this book, I wish to tell people that no task is unachievable, no obstacle is insurmountable, and there is no darkness that cannot be eliminated through light, given we have complete faith in God and His plans for us trust Him to be the best caretaker of our affairs. It takes a lot to believe but only a single moment of despair to throw away all hope and faith and resign yourself to a life of misery and regret. Without believing in the truth, we will only be led astray by those who claim to be 'leaders' but are mere phonies and hypocrites.

Chapter One - Leadership and Ethics

A lot of successful people credit their success to one quality: leadership. It is this quality that was common between all of God's messengers and their disciples. God created them to be leaders because without them possessing leadership qualities, they would not have been able to spread God's word, despite the demanding challenges they faced.

So, what does it mean to be a true leader? A true leader is one of a kind. They fight the wrong and stand by the right even when the entire world opposes them. A true leader shows faith and hopes even in the toughest of storms and waits for the dark to fade away with remarkable patience.

They have an indomitable spirit and face the cruelties of life with courage. Such people are not only looked up to by members of their families but also by their co-workers and others in their community.

It is the desire of every person who aims to be successful in life to have leadership qualities in them. A leader is self-sufficient and does not rely on depending on anyone else for help or support. They know how to look after themselves and do not hesitate to speak their mind. If we examine closely, each of God's messengers possessed the same characteristics. They were defenders of the truth, never shying away from introspection, reflecting on their habits and the elements informing their natures. One of these important elements is the morality of the individual, also known as 'ethical values. '

The reason why most companies fail to perform well is that they do not have a set of ethical values in place within their organizational structure. The moral values of an organization govern its behavior and culture. The culture, in turn, sets the tone for the way the employees and employers interact with each other. If the culture of an organization lacks strong ethical values, then the organizational system is sure to collapse.

A working environment free from any kind of toxicity ensures the success of the company as well as intellectual stimulation. When everyone working in a company feels secure and safe, they contribute efficiently to its overall growth and success.

A type of leader that enables others to perform their best is a 'transformational leader.' This type of leader helps his or her followers (or team players) to see the best in themselves and recognize their full potential. Thus, not only are the leader's ambitions and goals met by virtue of everyone on the team putting in their best, but the team players are also left feeling confident with a clear perspective as to how to best enact their roles under the leader's guidance. If you have a transformational leader in the form of your boss, you will have noticed how much you are willing to sacrifice your own interests to meet your boss's requirements.

Being a transformational leader does not only mean you enable your employees to give their best in the workplace but also allow them to make time for themselves whenever they ask for downtime and be flexible in your approach to carrying out business in order to build a healthy relationship with them. If, as an employee, you feel heard by your employer, then you have a healthy relationship with them based on the latter's true leadership and strong ethical values.

It is important that we go back to God in our discussion of true leadership and strong morals, as these were the foremost principles laid down by God when he sent his first two human creations to Earth. He taught Adam and Eve to be patient in their tough times and understand each other if they were to have a loving and respectful relationship. These qualities are universal and apply not only to the relationship shared between a husband and a wife but to every relationship that exists today and will exist tomorrow.

We realize that God is everywhere and present in everything that we do. We manifest God without realizing it. We manifest God when we give someone a helping hand or encourage or motivate someone to do better when they feel most dejected and distressed. Again, these are all qualities that are found in true leaders, and true leaders are a rarity in our world today. Thus, if we strive with sincerity in our hearts and ask God to make us the best of humans, then surely, he will guide us and show us the path of the righteous.

So far, we have looked at the emotional qualities that an individual should possess in order to be called a true leader, but now, we will look at some equally important and critical cognitive attributes. The ability to perceive change and adapt to it quickly, the ability to cater to the varying needs of your followers because each individual may have a separate problem that will need to be resolved.

The leader has to be decisive so as to be able to make quick decisions that serve not only them but also their followers.

They must be cooperative, persuasive where necessary, and socially skilled so that they can make contacts and, thus, stay updated about the current changes in their field of business.

Another important and necessary skill for a leader is their ability to freely, clearly, and effectively communicate their objectives or message to their followers. The message of the leader must have enough credibility to afford them a happy and satisfied audience. Nobody wants their message to be dismissed by listeners. In order to prevent that from becoming the case, the leader must communicate to his or her followers how their goals will also fulfill the goals of their followers. A give-and-take dynamic needs to be executed with the utmost care if the leader wishes to have dedicated and sincere followers.

Where necessary, leader must often sacrifice their own interests to fulfill those of their followers. This example of leadership is most commonly seen within families where the patriarch or matriarch bends so that the rest of the family members feel heard and safe.

A true leader takes responsibility and charge of the situation and, where necessary, bends the laws or rules of a workplace to accommodate the needs of the followers. It is imperative

Leadership: An Incumbent of Faith

that true leader makes good and not poor ethical choices if they really wish to succeed and prosper within the circles of their followers. This practice also applies to our political leaders who wish to secure loyal and dedicated followers and party members.

The people's overall interest should be considered if a political leader wishes to secure their position as a true leader. Of course, all of this brings us back to God, who has emphasized honesty and kindness as one of the most important qualities a human being can possess. Both of these qualities must also exist in a true leader.

The leader must also possess the precious quality of foresight and insight. They always plan one step ahead of their goals and objectives.

So, they are always planning ahead, thus making sure that if a crisis happens to befall them, they are in a secure position to make well-informed decisions and ones that do not put their followers' interests at risk.

Leadership goes a long way for the person who carries its qualities and for the ones who follow a leader; however, ethics must be considered as a key factor for genuine leadership.

Dr. Moses Haregewoyn

We've seen many historical figures who displayed leadership traits, but their intentions were not always pure or meant for their people's benefit.

Some used their charisma to manipulate others, such as Hitler and Stalin, leading to catastrophic results.

It is sometimes difficult for people to resist the charm, which leads them to blindly follow an individual. Charles Manson, an infamous figure that influenced his youthful followers to murder innocents, was known to have likable qualities that he used to draw the youth toward himself.

As a leader, you are always influencing others. However, if you're not mindful of how you exert this influence, it could lead to unforeseen consequences for yourself and your team.

Your ability to negatively impact someone's performance, or elevate it to new levels, is powerful and should be taken seriously. This is why ethics play a significant role in determining what makes an honest, reliable leader. Ethics are to leadership as mortar is to bricks.

Both are integral to one another, and together they create a strong foundation.

Leadership: An Incumbent of Faith

Ethics are what determine what is morally right or wrong. It is what helps us differentiate between the just and the unjust.

When we look at the prophets, they each carried the message of God and helped people differentiate between right and wrong.

These are things we take for granted today because humanity has evolved and seen many changes over the years, but even today, we find ourselves more polarized than ever before.

The reason why ethics play such a significant role in leadership is that we know that the person who chooses to take responsibility for his or her people is a reflection of his or her society.

Ethics are the reflection of the relationship between humans and nature.

How we interact with our environment indicates a sense of maturity and consideration. This contributes to an overall sense of human independence.

Since the beginning of recorded time, societies have been mostly primal and engaged in acts of violence, but when enlightened individuals – who eventually were proclaimed as prophets came along, they gradually enriched humanity.

Dr. Moses Haregewoyn

Those who were proclaimed as prophets illuminated paths for human improvement as well as tools to cultivate spiritual development, which, ideally, would have a civilizing and refining effect.

This independence – the potential within each of us- helps us make enlightened decisions.

Leaders are expected to be decisive, so without having a sense of right and wrong, they could risk muddling their entire situation, causing more harm than good.

This is why there is an insistence on ensuring that our people do not become corrupt.

It is easy to fall under the spells of our conditioning rather than rely on our own independent thinking.

If we strive to improve, our internal spell of ethics will be our driving force.

For leadership to function adequately, there must be an operational framework, and that is where ethics come into play. If a decision is made, there must be solid reasoning behind it.

Being ethical doesn't necessarily always mean following the law. It is true that the laws we set are rooted in ethical standards, but keep in mind that laws are prone to interpretation. Sometimes they can even deviate from what is deemed 'good.' Examples of this are America's pre-Civil War laws and South Africa's former apartheid laws.

Ethical behavior isn't limited to doing what society expects us to do either. History shows that following the herd is not always the best solution.

It takes guts to stand alone and believe in what is right. Otherwise, being swayed away can lead to mistakes such as the German people made during the Nazi regime.

Types of Ethics

Ethics are like a tree; it carries branches that work together to keep it growing and evolving.

The branches are offshoots of the main concern tree which are:

- Descriptive Ethics.

- Normative Ethics.

- Meta-Ethics.

- Applied Ethics.

Descriptive ethics refers to what 'people actually believe' or are 'made to believe' to be 'right or wrong' and holds up human actions as 'acceptable or not acceptable or punishable' by law.

As we know, laws evolve with time, which requires people to behave accordingly. This is why descriptive ethics are also referred to as 'comparative ethics' because there is a comparison between the customs of the past and present.

Normative ethics are the standards or the set of expectations on personal behavior. It is referred to as 'prescriptive ethics' as well because it relies on the principles which determine whether an action is 'right' or 'wrong.' The basic rule of this is 'doing to others as we want them to do to us.' Since no one wants to be hurt by someone else, they may choose not to do the same.

We don't want to be robbed, so we refrain from stealing. This framework provides justification for punishing a person who disturbs social and moral order.

Leadership: An Incumbent of Faith

Meta-ethics, also referred to as 'analytical ethics,' focuses on the origin of the ethical concepts themselves. Unlike the former ones, it does not focus on an action being good or bad. Instead, it questions what 'goodness' or 'rightness' is.

Think of it as an abstract way of approaching ethics. One might delve into the ones such as naturalism, non-naturalism, emotivism, and prescriptivism.

Naturalists and non-naturalists believe that moral language is cognitive and can be true or false. On the other hand, Emotivists believe that moral utterances cannot be cognitive. Instead, to them, morality consists of emotional expressions of approval or disapproval, and the nature of moral reasoning and justification needs to be reinterpreted. Prescriptivists have a similar approach, stating that moral judgments are prescriptions or prohibitions of action rather than facts about the world.

Applied ethics deals with more philosophical examination, mostly from a moral standpoint of certain matters in both private and public life. This generally applies to professions from different fields, such as doctors, teachers, politicians, and many more. The approach deals more with the rightness

Dr. Moses Haregewoyn

or wrongness of social, cultural, religious, and economic issues.

Chapter Two - The Seven *P's* of Leadership

Leading others tends to come in different forms; some choose to be strict and rigid, while others are calm and patient. There is no absolute manner that determines which is the best approach, but one trait tends to be common in all: they inspire.

When we think about the prophets who spread God's message, most were simple men living in very chaotic times. They often found themselves surrounded by a corrupt and unforgiving society.

Prophets challenged evil norms not necessarily by resorting to the sword but by displaying compassion and kindness. Jesus was known for his charitable acts. The prophet Muhammad was kind and forgiving, even to his enemies. Abraham, too, never held spite and wished the best for those who were harmed. On the other hand, there are those who lead with an iron fist.

Atatürk, the father of the Turks, led his country from being 'the sick man of Europe' to a modernized, progressive nation that changed the country's dynamic in Europe.

Dr. Moses Haregewoyn

Some led by their own example by the symbolism of the act they did. Nelson Mandela, who spent twenty-seven years in prison, refused to take revenge against the individuals who placed an unfair judgment on him. He understood that to ethically lead his people, he must set aside his personal feelings and push South Africa ahead by bringing an end to apartheid through cooperation and understanding.

Circumstances and personal nature play a role in creating the kind of leadership style one might take. If times are too harsh, then a hardened leader can emerge. However, if things are stable but people require guidance, then the leader is likely to be calm and flexible.

Leadership follows a structure: hierarchal and non-hierarchal. Organizations typically follow this model. In order to maintain workflow and accountability, a structure must have a strong foundation.

In a hierarchal approach, leadership employs a top-down pyramidal structure utilizing a narrow center of power that trickles down to its wider base of subordinates. Non-hierarchal, on the other hand, flattens the pyramid to form a structure of decentralized authority and lesser levels.

Leadership: An Incumbent of Faith

Hierarchal leadership structures can be functional or divisional. Functional hierarchal is arranged by functions that center on engineering or marketing. Non-functional is referred to as organic. It has a few layers, each of which reports to a single individual.

There is considerable debate about whether leadership skills are an innate talent or are traits that can be learned. Some believe one has to be born with them, which is why some people display leadership traits from an early age.

They tend to be the stars of the classroom or have a charm about them that draws those around them. Others take time to learn and develop these skills. You may remember someone who was shy during their younger years, but as they grew older, they inspired and motivated others.

Either way, since it is hard to differentiate between those in possession of innate leadership skills and those who can develop these skills over time, there are certain traits necessary to have when leading others.

They are referred to as the *seven* Ps of friendship and include the following:

- Purpose.

- Passion.

- Persistence.

- Presence.

- Patience.

- Pragmatism.

- Progression.

Having a few of these qualities is helpful, but attaining all will guarantee that others will enthusiastically follow you and help you achieve your goals.

Purpose refers to asking oneself a few key self-reflective questions: why? What is yours? Why? Why do you choose a particular agenda, or why are you choosing to fight for a cause? The answers are by no means easy. Reasoning can change and evolve over time because self-discovery is a never-ending process. This shouldn't mean you stop asking the question of why.

It is important to know the core reason. Otherwise, the individual risks being directionless and not having a fully self-aware nature. One person can detect when another person is unsure of themselves, which affects their level of trust. Not knowing the 'why' can even reduce self-esteem, leaving the person in a doubt-filled state.

Passion is one of the main driving forces not just behind leadership but in other aspects as well. A lot of people pick up the guitar because they dream of becoming a rock star. Yet, only the passionate ones are able to endure the long period of errors, cuts to their fingers, and constant practice till they finally learn the instrument. In leadership, having passion instills more drive into a person.

They are not leading people with a dull, dead, and cold nature. Instead, they display a zeal of enthusiasm that inspires and invigorates others. Passion does not have to be someone being overly emotional about their cause; it can be reflected in the hard and long work they put in to succeed.

Persistence is consistency. No matter how many times one falls, one gets back up again. Prophets experienced a considerable amount of discrimination and harm from those who opposed them, but they never gave up. Days were spent being pelted with stones, cruel words, and spiteful anger, yet the prophets never gave in. They were not only dealing with the common man but the rich & influential as well.

Dr. Moses Haregewoyn

Remember, talent, genius and education are, without a doubt, powerful tools, but there is no point in them without persistence.

Many people with skills tend to have weak spirits because they give up too easily. To combat this, real leaders do not let defeats get them down. They learn from their mistakes and keep striving forward. Those who forge ahead are the ones that make a difference.

Presence is the ability to have your aura felt within a room. When we talk about someone who stands out from a crowd or carries certain energy that draws everyone's eyes to them, that person has that presence. This doesn't require the person to be too loud or a show-off. You simply see and sense a person in complete control of themselves, and when it is their turn to speak, they dominate the room.

Patience is key. Everyone is familiar with the saying, 'good things come to those who wait.'

There is truth in this. In today's world, we've become a bit too accustomed to comfort with the immediacy of technology as it slowly grasps more of our time. This has made us impatient.

Leadership: An Incumbent of Faith

The younger generation is quick to surrender, which is why they become depressed easily.

Nothing in life comes easy. Those who accomplished tremendous feats, whether in science or arts, endured years of trial and error. Businessmen aren't made in a day; they go through many mistakes before learning how to run their organizations.

Pragmatism is a manner of dealing with problems or situations that focuses on practical approaches and solutions. The prior traits mentioned focus more on an emotional aspect, but leaders must also be realistic.

One can't keep tossing fancy words and rhetoric; one needs to display some form of action. It's a cliché to say, 'actions speak louder than words,' but this rings true.

When approaching matters pragmatically, it is important to look at the bigger picture, weighing out the pros and cons of any given decision before implementing it.

Progression is deemed a likable attribute among leaders, especially young ones. Our world is moving faster than ever before, and it is compulsory for everyone to look ahead.

Those whose thinking remains rigid and stuck in the past never get ahead in life. This is a challenging trait to acquire when comfort is common.

In our situation today, the general public isn't as driven or motivated as before. If one isn't pushing ahead, then they are bound to be left behind.

How Leadership Changed Over the Years

When the word 'leader' is mentioned, it's natural to assume a strong, autocratic, and charming personality, all embodied into one person. Nowadays, that is no longer the usual approach, save for a few exceptions. In general, the approach to leadership in the last many years has shifted from an autocratic style to a more collaborative approach, fostering teamwork, productivity, innovation, and creativity.

Keep in mind that the fundamental of leadership hasn't entirely changed. Those who wish to lead still need a vision that can be channeled into inspiration and commitment from others. Being honest, transparent, and having integrity still matters.

In the last two decades, most things were still relatively stable, and change was a slow, steady occurrence. Once the internet and technological advancement became more rapid and fast-growing, many fields struggled to keep up.

The days of autocratic leaders and managers passing on orders were slowly starting to fade away. The focus on hard skills and following orders to get tasks done wasn't adapting too well to the changing dynamics.

This automatically led to a change in how things were to be run going forward. From one person running the show, the emphasis switched to a more collaborative effort, one wherein there was fair exchange amongst a team. Work was no longer sent from above. Instead, it was created within a group.

Hard leadership style declined because the younger generation didn't take kindly to harsh orders and the 'do as I say' approach. What came about was a gentle approach to leadership, where leaders were more people-oriented than task-based. Kindness was preferred over a harsh tone. Empathy was appreciated, and selfishness was sidelined.

The aim of this was to get the best out of a team by using personality profiling that helped find effective ways to manage people on their natural behavioral preferences.

Dr. Moses Haregewoyn

Leaders do not participate in the old school approach of monitoring and guiding because remote working has become more prevalent, which gives a person some independence on how to go about doing their work.

Timeline of Leadership Evolving

People have been leading, mentoring, and guiding others for countless years, from the simple patriarch of the family to the tribal chief of a village. Their villages grew into cities. Chiefs became lords and kings. With time, countries were formed, and leadership positions like 'Presidents' and Prime Ministers came about. Even Prophets took upon these roles and set a precedent on how people should be treated and taken care of.

The styles of leadership were mostly a product of their time. Kings and rulers ran things with authority and an iron fist because the culture and requirements were such. Harsh conditions prevailed; hence, they elicited a doctoral approach. On the other hand, Prophets eschewed a more loving and kind approach that differed from the tyrants. Their belief was that, although life was cruel and challenging, kindness to others would bring the best out of people engendering a general sense of community.

Leadership: An Incumbent of Faith

With time, the agricultural revolution gave way to the industrial revolution. During the latter, the theory of the 'Great Man' was formulated. This presupposed that leaders were born to lead because they already held innate qualities and characteristics that made 'ruling' their destiny. Individuals in this category included figures like Napoleon, Alexander the Great, Genghis Khan, and others.

Individuals were counseled that in order to be a leader, one had to emulate the great men of the ancient past. This was a flawed approach due to its bias and lack of empirical data.

Then came the interregnum period. As the theory of the 'Great Man' declined, the focus honed more on the study of power. This is related to the amount of power acquired by a leader and the way the power is utilized to influence, persuade and control subordinates. At best, the scope of control was limited to 150 subordinates who would abide by the use of this theory, after which coercion and force would be used.

This approach ignored leadership personality. This theory became more prevalent after World War II when the world experienced seismic sociopolitical shifts and ushered in luminaries like Churchill, Stalin, Roosevelt, Mao, and others.

From 1945-1980 focus shifted towards the behavioral, situational, and contingent. Here the environment and circumstances became more important and how they affected leadership. The belief was that the leader mattered less than the environment where the leader-subordinate dynamic occurred. Leadership had become separated from the individual as a leader – now, it was a function by which large organizations could accomplish their goals. Those deemed successful leaders were the ones carrying strong adaptability.

Understanding why people do what they do is the foundation of all influence. When you are inaccurate in doing this, your attempt to influence others will have random and unpredictable effects. But people are complex, and as a leader, you don't have the time or resources to decipher everyone's psyche. The key is to know when and how to tailor your approach to understanding others in different kinds of interactions.

Recognizing adaptability as a key quality led to a considerable change in how leadership was conceptualized.

Leadership: An Incumbent of Faith

This was given the term 'contingency.' Success was based on factors including personality, behavior, influence, and situation. The roles of the leader and subordinate remained clearly delineated, with the leader directing and the subordinate following.

In the modern era, the focus is mostly on the leader and the qualities that gave rise to leadership. Key trait modalities include transformational, authentic, and servant.

Transformational leadership is when leaders and followers reciprocally help each other to increase motivation and ethical behavior. The burden of leadership rests upon all individuals within a group working towards a common goal. Change and adaptability are key to this method. This approach requires a charismatic leader whose vision can be conveyed to others, inspiring them.

Authentic leadership focuses on the veracity of a person in charge as well as their actual leadership. Here, leaders and followers focus on positive rather than negative traits. The needs of the followers are more important than the organization.

Servant leadership emphasizes the nurturing of subordinates. Here, the leader focuses predominantly on the people providing opportunities for followers to rise to the level of leaders.

Chapter Three - Pros & Cons of Leadership Styles

Autocratic leadership has been the most basic form of leadership for many years. Our species was forged by harsh conditions, with paths fraught with difficulty. Being surrounded by danger from various and often unpredictable sources such as animals, disease, natural calamities, cultural violence, and warfare - yet the will to survive was strong among people.

However, due to the tough nature of the environment, leaders had to be resolute - decisive to the point of being controlling. Their word was law, and there was no equivocating or questioning; these leaders took the form of tribal chiefs and kings, later evolving into dictators. Autocratic leadership, in terms of definition, is a top-down approach when it comes to all decision-making, procedures, and policies within any organization.

An autocratic leader doesn't focus much on gathering input from his team or followers. Instead, they tend to make executive decisions that they expect everyone to follow. It is mostly a one-man show. There are both benefits and problems with this style.

Pros

It can be an efficient system. Rather than wasting time debating and overthinking the best decision, autocratic leaders cut through the clutter and take decisive action. This gets things done in times of need and instills a sense of trust in the leader and followers.

It keeps the team cohesive and consistent when one person is taking charge. There is no confusion on who answers to who, which reduces conflict, and everyone is clear on their roles. They are delegated specific duties and do not cross boundaries that may hinder work.

Cons

Autocratic leadership can stifle creativity, collaboration, and innovation. Since there is no room for debate and discussion, new ideas and innovation are sidelined. There is no room for diversity either, so growth doesn't tend to take place.

It can lead to a disengaged and demotivated workforce because they feel undervalued. Under an autocrat, it is common to be belittled by your superior, which can affect loyalty between the leader and follower.

Autocratic leadership hinders any potential for a mentor-protégé dynamic as well. It is important for a system to have continuity for work to get done. However, without mentorship, there is no growth present, and professional evolution is hindered.

Transactional leaders, as we know, are defined by control, organization, and short-term planning. Leaders who adopt this style rely on a system of rewards and punishment to motivate their followers.

This resembles autocratic leadership, but it differs in that transactional leadership involves a clear exchange between the leaders and followers.

Pros

This approach is quite effective when it comes to reaching short-term goals. Hard work is incentivized through the promise of success.

There is a clear understanding of what kind of behavior is expected from team members due to the system of reward and punishment.

There is a set structure that maintains discipline and stability. Work can progress without being swayed.

Cons

Due to its similarity to autocratic leadership, the transactional style model suffers from similar problems, starting with limitations to creativity, growth, and initiative. This demotivates followers and can lead to employees having conflicts with their supervisors and managers.

A fleeting reward only provides temporary happiness and is not enough when long-term solutions are needed. Those who are not driven by extrinsic motivation will be unable to make an impact because they feel unheard and are not satisfied with the rewards being provided.

Bureaucratic Leadership relies on a clear chain of command, strict regulations, and confirmation by its followers. As the name itself suggests, this is a leadership style that's commonly found in government entities, as well as military and public organizations.

Pros

Leadership: An Incumbent of Faith

It is stable in terms of job security and outcomes. Since everything is procedural, everything is kept in check, and work flows smoothly.

It removes favoritism from the equation because everyone has a fixed set of tasks to do. No one stands out, and this reduces the chances of enmity and jealousy between workers.

The processes and regulations are highly visible, so the system is transparent. There are lesser chances of behind the scene deals, and everything is operated systematically without taking advantage of loopholes.

Cons

The bureaucratic system, especially today, is deemed inefficient as every single thing has to go through a chain of command. This process is slow and enduring, which hinders growth or productivity.

There is no encouragement for an individual's personal or professional growth, which can lead to the mundanity of work and a demotivated workforce.

It doesn't foster teamwork building or fostering collaboration within teams, so a sense of unity is always missing.

Changes and improvements are difficult to implement, leaving the system very redundant and unproductive.

Charismatic leadership is a management style wherein a leader uses communication skills, persuasiveness, and charm to influence others. Charismatic leaders use their ability to connect with people deeply, which can be essential to lead in times of crisis or help those struggling to progress.

Pros

The level of inspiration and motivation is very high. When people feel heard and understood on a deeper level by their leader, they are driven to be as helpful and effective as possible. This encourages a sense of camaraderie, collaboration, and unity amongst a team or followers.

This style tends to lead to a more positive change as it leaves room for discussion and debate. With everyone instilling ideas, innovative and forward-thinking solutions are formed.

Cons

Leadership: An Incumbent of Faith

Due to their charm and sphere of influence a charismatic leader possesses, there can be times when they become more focused on their own agenda than that of their people. Since these individuals have everyone under their influence, their people may follow orders blindly without properly questioning the moral implications of their actions.

This leadership style can also be seen as shallow and disingenuous. Since everything centers on a leader's personality and charm, there is more of a persona running the show rather than solid substance. This leads to figures adopting the correct style of addressing crowds, but they have little to no vision or plan on how to bring about change for the better.

Transformational leadership creates a vision based on identified needs and guides people toward that unified goal through inspiration and motivation. What differentiates this style from the others is that it focuses on changing dysfunctional systems and dysfunctional processes.

Pros

The approach can be highly motivating for people. Since change is encouraged, it welcomes people's perspectives and ideas as well as brings a sense of communal purpose.

Creativity and collaboration help keeps a team's spirit strong, and innovation is cherished.

Sturdy relationships are established, which allows individuals to maintain a sense of involvement. With a team strongly unified, results are achieved more efficiently and effectively. Followers and workers have more autonomy within the structure of their jobs. Instead of filling a subservient role and doing what they're told, the individual has a voice in how to achieve their tasks. With the transformational approach, the individual is given credit for the self-awareness and creativity to make their work easier.

Cons

This style of leadership does not necessarily work in all kinds of circumstances or setups. A bureaucratic workplace, for example, would not benefit from this kind of approach.

If anything, considering the differing culture of approach, it may create more errors in the process.

Since so much collaboration and input are given by employees, there is the inevitability of a clash or conflict of interest. Not everyone will always agree on the same thing, and that can make it difficult to make a unanimous decision.

Leadership: An Incumbent of Faith

The constant conflict, if not handled well, may lead to a disruption of the status quo. The leader might find him or herself being challenged altogether, weakening unity and progress for the organization.

Coaching leadership emphasizes collaboration, support, and guidance. The intent of this leadership model is to bring the best out of people by making people work on tasks that will have challenging obstacles. The aim is to make sure they are driven to their fullest potential in order to achieve their goal.

Pros

This style encourages two-way communication and collaboration that establishes trust and mutual understanding. Creating an environment that fosters open communication can go a long way to strengthening team dynamics.

The coaching approach encourages free-flowing constructive feedback. Instead of yelling and blaring negative criticism, there is a proper manner of sitting someone down and helping that person understand their strengths and weaknesses. This can help fix what is wrong and improve upon other qualities.

41

Dr. Moses Haregewoyn

It is a leadership style that facilitates personal and professional development. Instead of helping someone for the short term, they are given the benefit of knowledge and skills that will help them for a long time.

With the coaching model, the focus is on being supportive rather than judgmental. A worker can feel demotivated if they are criticized for their failings, but by helping them to improve, a sense of camaraderie is formed.

Cons

This style is time-consuming & resource intensive. Not everyone can make a good coach. It takes patience and energy, and sometimes flawed advice is passed on. It is not a fast or necessarily efficient approach because personal dynamics matter. Not everyone can always be on the same page, which potentially leads to misunderstandings and conflict.

A leader cannot give every single person advice all the time, and there can be a clash of expectations. This approach is not suitable either in high-pressure situations or strictly results-driven places. Democratic leadership, also referred to as participative leadership, is about letting multiple individuals participate in the decision-making process. This type of leadership is practiced in schools and even government systems.

Leadership: An Incumbent of Faith

Pros

This style encourages collaboration, teamwork, and a sense of unity within a group. Everyone relies on each other, allowing room for debate. It is a system of checks and balances that lends itself to more positive outcomes. If an error is made, the responsibility does not fall upon one person but is shared. In case one feels demoralized, he or she has the support and understanding of those leading alongside them.

The democratic model allows diversity - an inclusion of ideas, opinions, and ways of thinking. Approaching decisions in one repetitive manner can make the result generic and redundant. To be innovative, new thoughts and ideas need to be brought to the table, and democratic leadership allows that.

With more group engagement, the productivity level rises tremendously. An enthusiastic team that is united and dedicated can always outdo the work of a team that is simply following instructions and being generic in its approach.

With different ideas meshed together, the results can be more creative in nature. This establishes new and improved tactics that can overcome many hurdles with one swing.

Dr. Moses Haregewoyn

Since the responsibility for the decision does not entirely rest upon one person, there's no animosity or frustration between the decision-makers. Everyone is heard, and their opinions are brought to the table. Hence, whichever decision is agreed upon is always supported by the majority.

Cons

Despite its inclusive nature, there are certain problems with this style. Those who carry a minority opinion tend to be overridden. If a team of five leaders was asked to make a decision, where three went with one approach, but two demanded another, the conflict would ensue. However, since three obviously exceeds two, the decision would be decided by a majority in the end. If the result of the decision comes out bad, then the two who were against it would find themselves still sharing the responsibility and blame for going alongside a wrong decision.

When more than one person is involved in the decision-making process, it can lead to communication gaps, and confusion will surely follow. Communication is a vital aspect of leadership, as mortar is to a brick. Sometimes not everyone's in synch because people communicate and receive information differently. If there is a group involved in decision-making, then their differences in communicating with one another will come at a great cost. A misunderstanding could risk making the proper decision altogether.

Making a decision itself will take time. Since everyone has a say in the matter, it costs time, as disagreements are common. Action cannot be taken unless the decision is unanimous.

Sometimes those present in leadership positions aren't entirely trained or skilled as required. This poses a problem because their inexperience may end up causing more harm than good.

Collaborative leadership focuses on encouraging people to work together across functional and organizational boundaries. Its purpose is to allow collaboration with other teams and departments to accomplish shared goals.

Pros

This crossing-the-boundary approach allows creative, innovative ways of thinking. People exchange ideas, always allowing room to learn and implement something new. There's room for more opportunity in the process. By collaborating, sometimes, new forms of teams are made, leading to better teamwork and morale.

The level of trust is strengthened as well. In case someone from one department cannot find a solution to a problem in his own team, he can reach out to another. They have faith in one another's ability to establish stronger relationships.

Cons

Since boundaries are crossed, the blurred lines can cause ambiguity in roles and responsibilities. It becomes difficult to tell who bears responsibility for any given decision.

Sometimes the conflict caused can be more problematic because arguments and fights are no longer limited to an isolated group but spread over many departments. This can damage relationships within more groups, hence weakening the structure and spirit of teamwork.

There may be power struggles between leaders. Since responsibility is delegated over different departments, competition may arise and, unless healthfully tempered, can cause animosity between factions.

Servant leadership puts the needs and well-being of the followers first. The leaders who adopt this style have a very

Leadership: An Incumbent of Faith

'serve-first' approach which is aided by a growth mindset to prioritize their organization, employees, followers, and community above themselves. The people always come first, and the leader deems themselves answerable to them rather than the other way around.

Pros

Since the people are the first priority, a leader places emphasis on the development and betterment of others. This instills a strong sense of trust between the leadership in charge and their followers.

By investing effort into the development of others, there is room for improved performance, innovation, and collaboration. This results in a strong united team willing to take on the obstacles that inevitably arise.

The servant model creates a safe environment where people aren't afraid to make mistakes or stumble. Most people are generally scared to disappoint their leaders, but in this case, since the focus is more on making things better for people, it allows trial and error to occur, and both parties learn from one another.

There is less turnover and disengagement. People generally feel unwanted when they are reprimanded or when their needs don't seem to matter. In this style, since the people are the priority, both parties go the extra mile to make things better, and there is an uninhibited pipeline of communication between the followers and their leaders.

Cons

Putting the needs of the people first can be physically and mentally tiring work. People tend to become pressurized when their needs aren't being met, putting further strain on the leader in the process. Most servant-styled leaders experience burnout and exhaustion in the process. This, in turn, hinders work and makes way for errors and delays.

This approach is quite resourced and intensive but can be problematic when people are inexperienced or untrained. Without the right kinds of resources, the whole process of getting work done can fall apart.

The approach of placing people first does not necessarily fit well with everyone in a leadership position. It is difficult to train others in a serve-first mindset because some leaders may feel that due to their hard work and consistency, they should also be given additional credit and attention.

Leadership: An Incumbent of Faith

Some leaders feel that the people do not always know what they want and tend toward mob mentality, so it is imperative that authority lies with the one in charge.

Due to this approach's inherent inclusivity, many individuals may not be unified in the overall vision. This divide within their working populace poses a problem for the leader because the leader may have difficulty deciding which voice to listen to. It costs time, and it takes longer to achieve results.

Sometimes this style can be seen as 'weak.' If a leader is constantly listening to the whims of the people and being overly obedient, he or she can be seen as someone who lacks a backbone, is too subservient, and doesn't have a mind or vision of their own. This weakens faith and trust, and the leader can start to lose followers altogether.

Laissez-faire leadership takes a hands-off approach to leadership and gives others the freedom to make decisions. Leaders still provide their teams with the needed resources and tools, but they tend to remain uninvolved in the day-to-day work. This is usually used in creative settings such as advertising agencies and startups where independent thinking is encouraged.

Dr. Moses Haregewoyn

Pros

It empowers people to practice their own style of leadership. This helps form leaders and allows them the opportunity to learn from their mistakes. Relations are strengthened, and unity is forged.

The flexibility of this approach can create a more relaxed environment that can foster creativity and innovation.

There is less fear of failure because an error or mistake made does not always have to face administrative action. Within this more casual setting, there is little need for harsh punitive action, which keeps the atmosphere calm and steady.

A casual approach to work facilitates better relations between team members and their leader because the workers have been given a sense of independence, and they can always seek out help from their leaders in times of need.

Cons

Due to the slow and casual approach, there can be issues of low productivity. Tasks take too long, and attention to detail declines, leading to weaker results.

The leaders' absence at times weakens discipline and morale.

Conflicts between team members become more common. If a sole authority figure isn't present, team members may start jockeying for authority, which often leads to conflict.

As this sort of workplace is self-determined, with outputs varying from person to person, there is potential for missed deadlines or work piling up and overall productivity suffering.

This method cannot function if the team is unskilled and/or demotivated. Both aspects are determined by a leader, and their absence weakens the structure and drive of a team.

Different Management Systems and Styles

Any form of organization or working group to perform optimally requires not just an effective style of leadership but a strong management system as well.

Usually, leaders are confined to being one person or, at best, up to five, but there is a long, vast, and complex hierarchy below them that needs to be maintained vis morale and productivity.

Without a chain of command, leaders will have a hard time passing down directives and data, and the workload can become burdensome.

This places an important responsibility on managers to ensure that the work is being done systematically and everyone's output is both effective and efficient.

This, in turn, leads to the formation of management systems that highlight the dynamics present and the characteristics that are built around interactions between individuals.

The four management systems are:

- Exploitative authoritative.

- Benevolent authoritative.

- Consultative.

- Participative.

Exploitative authoritative models are extremely hierarchal in nature, where power and responsibility lie at the higher levels within an organization.

Individuals that are positioned lower in the hierarchy (non-managers) do not have any influence in the decision-making process and are not involved in the process by their superiors. This is usually due to a lack of trust between managers and employees. Communication is delivered top-down, and roles are dictated rather than being a two-way conversation. Higher management considers themselves responsible for achieving the goals and objectives but will hold employees responsible for any errors and mistakes made at the lower levels.

This approach has its perks because everything is done strictly, and all the roles and responsibilities are made plain and clear to the workers. However, due to the rigidness of the system, employees can start participating in counter-productive behavior since they feel unheard. The lack of communication is minimal, leading to errors and mistakes. Motivation is not inspired but, instead, forced through instilling fear or threat of punishment.

Benevolent authority is a management system where responsibility lies in the upper echelons of the organization. However, unlike authoritative, where performance is forced through the threat of punishment, employees are instead motivated through a reward system. Superiors place more trust in their employees and are more willing to give rewards to those who display good performance. There is steady two-way communication between employees and their managers, although upward communication is more limited to positive to neutral information, not queries or requests. Employees are not expected to give any suggestions or new ideas but, rather, maintain a subservient role.

This approach does delegate decision-making to the middle managerial level, so ideally, there are better leader and manager relations. The level of trust could be an improvement if managers avoid relating to subordinates in a condescending manner. However, the benevolent authoritative model still has its flaws because communication remains limited, which often leads to miscommunication and errors.

Competition can arise among team members who want to win the reward, which weakens unity and teamwork. For the most part, this approach is similar to authoritative, utilizing a prevailing promise of a reward instead of a threat of punishment. This method may be found lacking if employees feel demotivated, which can lead to increased turnover rates.

Consultative management systems place greater trust in their employees and subordinates. One key manner they accomplish this is by implementing ideas or beliefs that they share with their team members. This lets many of the workers feel involved, and the display of trust strengthens unity and teamwork spirit. There is an open level of communication throughout the hierarchy of the workplace. Team members are often consulted during the decision-making process, especially when it concerns any changes that will affect them substantially. Nonetheless, the ultimate decision-making power remains with those at the highest levels.

Employee motivation is fueled by incentives, including rewards and the possibility of involvement or even responsibility for specific tasks. In this system, employees are given greater freedom. Their involvement in meaningful tasks is used to boost intrinsic motivation.

This approach carries more benefits than the former two because communication is smoother, and motivation is generally higher. Cooperation is valued, and discussion can happen horizontally or even vertically. Responsibility is shared; hence, no one feels overburdened with work, and there is always someone to help out.

The participative management system is deemed to be the most satisfying for lower-level employees. Upper management places their full trust in their subordinates and actively works with them as part of the decision-making process. Employees have the freedom to discuss any issues or ideas with their administrators, knowing full well that feedback may be conducive to at least some kind of change.

Giving out rewards is very common, and teams cooperate with no direct competition between employees. The level of communication is very high, both horizontally and vertically, and teamwork is regular. The structure of the organization is generally flatter or smaller, containing lower hierarchical tiers, though it may be employed within any company.

When we observe these management models, it is clear that although they differ in the manner of their approach, each of them places emphasis on traits that establish their distinction from one another. These traits are motivation, leadership, communication, influence, and decision-making.

Motivation can be used both positively and negatively through rewards and incentives or by threats and punishment. Exploitative and Benevolent models utilize motivation through means of punishment, while Consultative and Participative lean more toward giving rewards; however, it is not necessary that each system is dedicated to solely one approach. In practice, leaders have to merge these models together from time to time.

Rewards generally come in the form of monetary bonuses, extra responsibility, opportunities for development, or the improvement of employee relationships with superiors.

Leadership styles play an influential role in management systems. These are highly variable and include different types, such as autocratic, servant, authentic, situational, transactional, and transformational leadership. Each of them has an impact on management at both higher and lower levels of an organization.

In any field of work, communication is key, and how it is utilized is incredibly enlightening with regard to the way power and authority are distributed throughout an organization. In an exploitative authoritative system, communication is entirely one-way, with decisions being dictated from higher management to subordinates, whereas in Participative systems, communications are horizontal, with employees being involved in the day-to-day decision-making process.

The levels of influence employees hold can be indicative of the managerial system employed. In Benevolent and Exploitative Authoritative systems, subordinates are generally not consulted regarding many decisions, even those that relate to their role. Whereas in Participative systems, employees are actively encouraged to take part in discussions about the business, some of which may influence the direction of the organization and their stance towards, hierarchically speaking, lower-tier workers.

In decision-making, when employees are asked their opinions and ideas regarding the running of the business, they may indirectly influence the decision-making of their superiors, with their thoughts, ideas, and values being included in any strategic planning.

However, in Authoritative systems, the final decisions are made by individuals at the upper levels of the organizational hierarchy. Alternatively, in Consultative systems, the employees are given a voice in the decision-making process through consultation, and in a Participative system, subordinates may have as much influence in decision-making and goal-setting as their manager.

Just as there are structures of management, there are also certain styles that need to be adhered to when running operations and delegating responsibilities to the employees. Management is by no means an easy task; instead, there is frequent communication involved, and proper expertise is required to maintain a smooth flow of work. This makes it imperative for the management style to be well-adapted to the nature of the organization.

There are six types of management styles to adhere to:

- Commanding.

- Visionary.

- Affiliative.

- Democratic.

- Pacesetting.

- Coaching

Commanding management includes a manager that takes full charge and invites no contrary opinions-their motto is 'my way or the highway.' Executives who use this tactic demand full power and authority over their employees and maintain discipline with the threat of punishment. It is not deemed to be the most effective approach, but it still holds influence over employee behavior.

The advantage of this is that managers have total control. However, it's hindered by the fact that over a long-term period, the lack of autonomy and creativity among employees creates a negative impact on the culture and atmosphere.

This style of management is effective in times of crisis, but once the matter is dealt with, it doesn't serve its purpose well. It is better to switch to a more cooperative style of management afterward.

Visionary management relies on a person's ability to mobilize people toward a goal. This is usually done using persuasion, charisma, and having a high emotional IQ. Those who practice this style of management can articulate a vision for the future and the path others must take to reach it. This style of management is effective when the manager is an authoritative expert in their field of work and a new fresh outlook is needed.

Leadership: An Incumbent of Faith

They leverage this expertise to gain respect and credibility in order to rally employees to follow them. Visionary management is less effective when employees are underdeveloped or require more guidance.

Affiliative management follows the motto of 'people first, task second.' The main objective of this style is to build relationships and create harmony within the organization. This model can have a positive impact on the work environment, but it has limits. It is easy and quick to recognize good work, but when someone is underperforming, then managers tend to shy away.

A manager adopting this strategy risks leaving the impression that mediocre performance is acceptable. Thus, the overall team output can deteriorate. These managers are good at keeping the environment upbeat and positive, but they do not perform well in a time of crisis.

Democratic management is generally seen in politics. In the workplace or other forms of organizations, a democratic management style allows everyone an equal say in building commitments and consensus among team members. This approach allows more participation in the decision-making process than commanding, autocratic management styles. It motivates employees by making them believe their opinion counts. In return, the worker will feel more committed to achieving the goals and objectives of the organization.

There are drawbacks to this style, especially when the workers are unskilled or untrained. To make effective decisions, expertise is needed. Another flaw in this approach is that it proves time-consuming as everyone's opinions are taken into consideration. This style of management does not serve well in a time of crisis.

Pacesetting managers have a 'do it yourself' approach. Most of the time, they prefer to finish the tasks themselves, which in turn sets a high standard of excellence that 'sets the bar.' They exemplify the behavior they want from their employees and do not hesitate to take over in situations where the worker is underperforming or behind schedule.

Democratic management can be effective in workplaces that are highly motivated and competent and requires little direction or coordination.

This model can be ineffective when a team requires additional development or coaching to accomplish goals with which they may develop their individual careers.

Leadership: An Incumbent of Faith

New employees who are inexperienced can feel overwhelmed by the demands for excellence which reduces morale.

Coaching management carries the primary objective of long-term professional development.

Managers who are chosen for this have a genuine interest in seeing others improve and helping them develop their strengths.

This style of management often provides abundant returns but isn't typically used because of the time and effort involved in investing in others.

It can be an effective approach when developing a talented workforce, but there are issues with it as well.

If managers find themselves in a challenging situation where employees are resistant to change and disinterested in professional development, then the style of management becomes ineffective.

Global Village

Although they interacted with one another, the nations and empires of antiquity were generally compartmentalized in terms of understanding cultures and economies outside of their region, i.e., geographically distant places were something of a mystery.

As of today, someone sitting in the far corner of Australia would be well informed about what is going on in the Middle East. Whether it is through media or frequent travel, the age of isolationism is long gone.

Our world today has not only experienced tremendous changes in the last hundred years but is now constantly changing at a rapid speed. A piece of technology that was improved over a period of years is now improved in a matter of months.

The way we connect with others has not only brought us closer but changed the way we perceive the world as well. Our planet has been described as a global village where boundaries have become blurred when it comes to communication and relationships. No matter where we are physical, we can pull out our phones and connect with anyone anytime, anywhere.

The term 'global village' was first coined by Marshall McLuhan in the early 1960s. McLuhan was a Canadian philosopher who specialized in media theory. He noticed how economies and politics were slowly becoming more intertwined, and trade had expanded tremendously across the world.

In the 21st century, this term refers to the way various media and technologies have accelerated the rate and frequency of social interaction, an impetus for cultural change everywhere. Most communicators and educators have adopted it to promote global awareness and understanding among students.

The concept of a global village is that we are no longer separate entities but interconnected parts of a larger community where knowledge, culture, languages, and even lifestyles have merged into one. This unique change from an isolated world to an interconnected one has its benefits and problems.

The benefits are:

- Interconnectedness.

- Togetherness.

- Job opportunities.

- Business.

- Diversity.

- Cultural awareness.

- Shared knowledge.

- Progress.

- Access.

- Global support.

Interconnectedness gives people opportunities to interact and learn from each other's experiences, knowledge, and cultures. It provides the opportunity to think differently than ever before. The possibilities are endless, as we have the ability to connect with others across countries instantly to find new ideas, thoughts, and solutions to solve problems.

Global awareness has surfaced through the slow and gradual removal of geographical boundaries, which has weakened pervasive language and cultural barriers that once hindered communication between people around the world. People can now share their hobbies, skills, and other passions, and there is always something new to learn.

Leadership: An Incumbent of Faith

Interconnectedness is the basis for peace and prosperity for all nations around the world. It's what makes us truly human and distinguishes us from other species.

Job opportunities are more plentiful than ever before. Now, a person is not limited to working only in their neighborhood, but they can move/travel to another country and work there. Additionally, the number and specialization of jobs have increased, expanding options for meaningful employment.

Business opportunities have increased as well, and with the onset of COVID-19, people are working remotely, sometimes from great distances from their particular headquarters. The World Wide Web has expanded in ways that many didn't expect. By connecting with others abroad, people have better chances of fulfilling their dreams. There are more chances of finding potential clients and business partners.

Diversity has been embraced much more in recent years due to globalization. People from different backgrounds of race, religion, gender, abilities, and even personalities now work together to achieve common goals. It has been deemed to be one of the most effective ways to help people achieve their full potential. This allows room for creativity, innovation, and an exploration of unique solutions through different perspectives.

Cultural awareness refers to familiarity with a variety of cultural traditions, practices, attitudes, customs, and beliefs. Tolerance is an important component of cultural awareness. It's not easy to always accept different cultures and ways of life, but learning to tolerate differences promotes understanding and acceptance of others. This strengthens unity and a sense of belonging.

Knowing how to communicate with people from different backgrounds helps an employee move up the ladder and establish better working relations. It provides an advantage that others cannot always have.

Shared knowledge is the sum of human experience and erudition. It shows in our collective intelligence. It's the intelligent, organized, and cumulative accretion of human knowledge, including facts, concepts, principles, and theories, as well as heuristics, which can be used to solve problems or create opportunities.

Leadership: An Incumbent of Faith

As social beings, we're nurtured by human contact, and we depend upon companionship and conversation, so, in many ways, shared knowledge is a human 'need.'

We want to be informed about the world around us, and in some cases, we need to know that our knowledge is shared by others.

Progress has been made possible at a faster rate because new technologies have helped pave the way for it. We know much more about the world and can make better-informed decisions.

We are, in fact, evolving on a societal level as we learn more about communication, technology, public health, economics, civil society, and even foreign policy.

Access has come about much easier than before. Our interconnectedness has opened up avenues of unlimited possibilities. It has even brought us new challenges along with opportunities, such as our connection to people, environment, information, and opportunities – to name a few. Although the sheer volume of information, services, and concepts can be overwhelming, their utility cannot be denied.

Global support has made helping others easier and faster. When a natural disaster occurs, the clean-up and reconstruction efforts don't rest solely on the locals but, rather, are shared by the world community.

Aid, financial assistance, and medical supplies come rushing in. The United Nations has played a pivotal role in helping countries in need, whether financially or socially. Experts are sent to help solve a crisis.

When war breaks out, countries have a better chance of coming to a negotiating table with third-party intervention.

Cons

With every benefit, there is also a price. Becoming a global village has helped us tremendously, yet this connectivity is not without its issues.

These include:

- Isolation.

- Stress.

- Lifestyle.

- Lack of privacy.

Leadership: An Incumbent of Faith

- Greed.

- Misinformation.

- High competitiveness.

- Reduced awareness.

The process of becoming a global village has pushed the world to change at a pace that can be quite difficult to keep up with. Machines and technology are updated on a yearly basis, but with people, there is a slow, steady process of learning, growing, and maturing with experience and time. This disconnect has led to a series of problems, especially for the younger generation.

In isolation, the fast pace has created something of a paradox. Our ability to connect with others is unprecedented, yet, in the developed world, loneliness is epidemic in a way we haven't seen. This isn't a result of the absence of family and friends, but rather, we've become slaves to communication technology, a force that keeps our minds preoccupied, making it difficult to build real, long-lasting relationships with others.

Everyone's glued to their phones (or other forms of electronic communications) which leads to a lack of participation in real-time human interaction. These exchanges have the potential to enrich our lives and bring joy. How can anyone achieve intimacy with another person when they are constantly scrolling through social media?

Stress levels have escalated exponentially. Since the pace of growth is faster than our ability to keep pace, we find ourselves working longer and harder to the point of exhaustion.

Daily, many of us battle stressors- we experience work-related stress, relationship stress, financial stress, and maybe even a fear of missing out. To be connected to so much stimulus all the time can engender a feeling of dread for a variety of reasons, from a sense of being overwhelmed by the bombardment of too much information to a sense that we are somehow being excluded from something important. It has become difficult for individuals to avoid certain formidable issues, and this can lead to high anxiety.

People are, in fact, losing sleep because they spend hours scrolling through social media.

Lifestyle has been affected by the growing interconnectivity of the world. Since our attention has been diverted to digitally-based platforms, people tend to invest more money and time in technology. This can become quite expensive, and other areas of our lives are affected, such as relationships and physical health, because we prioritize those over 'comfort.'

Another problem with this is that technology can easily distract us. The average attention span has reduced in recent years, and people find it difficult to focus. Appreciation has gone more toward the virtual than the physical.

Our privacy has become a target for hackers. There are those who aren't comfortable having their private matters put in the digital space, but sometimes, without their consent, this content is still published.

This hyperconnected environment contains an enormous wealth of data collected by companies. What we say, who we talk to, where we go, what we buy, how much money we make, and so many other things are recorded and saved somewhere in databases. Lines are crossed because there is a difference between something that is intentionally made available online and something that shouldn't be but could, nonetheless, be seen in real-time. As a result, private information can be abused – up to and including blackmail.

Dr. Moses Haregewoyn

With so many options available to us, it is natural for us to want more. This, however, if left unchecked, manifests in greed. Corporate companies have been causing tremendous damage to natural resources for profit's sake. A desire for attention leads people to partake in controversial antics on social media. Some see their peers having fun, feel left out, then start investing in the same endeavors without considering them rationally. Greed automatically leads to excess, and overconsumption never helps anybody.

Misinformation has become common. People can put up misleading content, which can affect behaviors and mass opinions, generating misperceptions and, in extreme cases, harm. When it comes to vetting the accuracy of information provided over the web, it seems there's no uniform system of checks and balances. Common wisdom states that bad news travels faster than good. As we see, it's common for false, especially sensationalistic, information to spread exponentially in this connected world.

Information can be misused by those with an agenda. Their information might be based on fact, but how it is presented can be altered and misconstrued. We saw this during the pandemic when conspiracy theories about vaccinations spread like wildfire. This not only spread panic but cast aspersions upon the collected body of research produced by scientific communities across the globe.

Even though job opportunities have increased and people have the means to work remotely in a worldwide marketplace, it has made competition greater than before. There are currently over 4.5 billion users on the internet, making too many candidates available for too few jobs. Hiring has become more challenging, which is why many companies have created a series of tests to effectively sift the unqualified from a sea of applicants.

Competition for jobs is not the only thing that has escalated, but competition, in general, has risen. Now companies from Asia are competing against companies in the West.

The excessive push to win, and be ahead of the others, leads to issues of deforestation, excessive consumption, and even bankruptcy.

Companies spend millions to sell their product without taking into account how their behavior is affecting their balance sheets.

Dr. Moses Haregewoyn

Natural resources are consumed without an effective system of checks and balances. This harms our environment and, by proxy, degrades our quality of life.

Economic recessions have occurred many times because of overproduction. The recent 2008 crash was a result of banker/lender overreach in the real estate market.

They lacked the assets to back their obligations, and their blind greed- coupled with a wanton intention to stay ahead of the competition- cost them in the end.

Scores of people lost their jobs, and many were forced to the streets - either in ruin or searching for gainful employment. Even now, despite the passage of time, there remain those seeking work, hoping to make ends meet for their families.

It's ironic that the internet has helped us become more aware of what is happening around the world, but with such a barrage of information, it can be hard to differentiate fact from fiction.

We can lose sight of what is important in the process. The large amounts of content have also desensitized us.

It is common for us to feel bad about some tragic incident, but when we see it frequently, we don't feel as emotionally attached because, soon enough, some other tragedy garners our attention.

Even the things we see on the internet are specifically designed to give us what is suitable for our needs rather than providing an overall picture.

Remote Leadership

Leadership styles vary, and at times it can become difficult to interpret which is the most effective manner in which to lead. In recent years, a new form of leadership has emerged. It's called 'remote leadership.'

Remote leadership is currently a growing concept in global companies. It is seen as flexible and can take in elements of traditional leadership styles alongside elements of Agile methodologies to lead distributed teams. Despite its growing popularity, most leaders and managers are not quite sure how to utilize it. To reap the benefits of distributed work, leadership needs to be tackled as a foundational part of the hybrid and remote workplace.

Communication is a big hurdle for remote leaders. Leaders used to be co-located in offices, and managing via in-person interactions can struggle with asynchronous communication.

Dr. Moses Haregewoyn

The fact that they can't always get instant replies from a remote worker is a source of frustration for some.

A successful remote leader learns to be accessible when working asynchronously and tries to build a safe environment in the digital sphere, regardless of the physical distance. When communication happens asynchronously, 'information fidelity' is lower, and there's a greater risk of miscommunication due to the lack of body language.

There are skills that are valued in remote leadership that center around active listening, remaining in touch with a team, being around for informal moments, and making room for discussion amongst the team.

Some of the qualities of an effective remote leader include the following:

- *Dynamism:* Virtual teams follow leaders who actually do the work of getting projects done. Dynamic remote leaders help other team members with tasks, as well as keep a team on schedule and goal-oriented.

- *Motivation:* Successful remote leaders understand they need to take a different approach to make things happen. They use collaborative, communicative approaches to improve accountability and transparency.

- *Flexibility:* Remote leaders need to be flexible enough to accommodate uncertainty and the changing requirements of different workers. Successful remote leaders are also capable of nimbly adjusting their leadership approaches to multiple situations.

- *Trust:* Remote work isn't possible without trust. A successful remote leader trusts that workers will complete their job and they will be able to communicate if there are roadblocks or issues with the projects.

Being a remote leader isn't necessarily easy, but it can be accomplished through a series of following steps. To be an effective remote leader and create a more decentralized comfort zone, the following things are necessary:

- Time management.

- Staying connected.

- Be content with letting go.

- Overcommunicate.

Time management plays an important role in remote leadership because those who have full clarity on who does what, when, and where one can find finished work or work in progress have a good understanding of what is going on and knows where effort needs to be implemented. In case something is wrong, then help can be provided.

If there is too much to do and a person feels overworked, there is still a clear start and end time for the day and plans for sufficient breaks. This helps relieve some level of stress and makes the workers feel valued, making them work more efficiently.

Since remote work is associated with social isolation, it is important to stay connected. Within a glut of isolation, members can start to feel alienated or unnecessary. People may miss interacting with colleagues. Without interaction, loneliness can intensify, which consequently affects work productivity negatively.

This is why it is good to schedule group chats and have joint lunch sessions with the team. Seeing the leader make these small, kind gestures help improve morale and boosts productivity in the workforce.

Remote work, in itself, is quite challenging. Working from home, distractions can be more of an issue; an increase in production errors may be the result of this diffused focus.

The work toll itself can become overwhelming, which is why as a leader, it is okay to let some things go. Rather than constantly holding on to authority, it is better to delegate responsibility to others. When employees see that their leader trusts them to do the work, it improves their morale, and a strong sense of trust is established.

Leaders have to make some time for themselves; otherwise, work stress will get the better of them.

Since isolation is a common characteristic of remote leadership, strong emphasis needs to be placed on communication.

Talking to others is important, not writing instructions, but talking to them. The face-to-face approach; for the remote worker- has a stronger bonding effect.

Dr. Moses Haregewoyn

An employee would feel valued when their boss wishes to speak to them directly rather than sending generic emails and notes.

Not only should the nature of communication be direct, but the amount has to be timely and consistent.

Since the individual is not present physically, misunderstandings may occur, and the margin for error increases.

Giving basic instruction isn't enough. There must be that steady exchange of interaction. The leader must ensure that no information is overlooked or too vague.

The nature of 'over-communication' helps bring the team together because everyone has the opportunity to say what they want, leaving no room for ambiguity, animosity, or frustration. Complaints regarding the workplace may be shared, which helps employees brainstorm and/or vent constructively.

Chapter Four - Religious Systems and Leadership Patterns

There is a certain irony to how far the Western world has come. We have managed to make scientific breakthroughs, fought countless wars against tyranny, created a unique and innovative technology, and led the way for many social movements. Yet, despite all these accomplishments, the people couldn't be further away from religion itself.

People performing acts of worship have declined considerably over the last many years, and attention appears to be drifting more and more towards individualism and personal gratification. We tend to look at religion as if they are made-up stories and overlook the fact that it was them that helped us establish ethics, morals, values, and systems that kept our society grounded and together. The laws in our constitutions stem from the teachings of the prophets who came and went.

How is it that the incredible wisdom of the prophets, which has survived for so many years, is no longer viewed as something viable in the modern world? Our societies can champion their developments, but the rise rates of suicide, depression, loneliness, divorce, and mental health clearly show that our deviation from worship and spirituality has weakened our resolve in the world. People feel unfulfilled while they work day to day, a sense of purposelessness pervading their thoughts.

Factor this spirit of pointlessness in with the boredom that rote tasks may foment, and we can begin to understand why people resort to different forms of addiction, be it drinking, smoking, or scrolling through social media. Those vices are not the cure. They are the only means to encourage escapism.

Religious systems gave us what many of our ancestors did not fully understand, norms and values. Bringing a feeling of togetherness and protecting one another. Take a look at the ten commandments. Each and every one of them can be seen, using slightly different verbiage, within our human rights laws. 'Thou shall not kill' is the core tenet that led to punishment against acts of murder and harm. There are many more to follow. Religious systems thoroughly outline how one should behave in public, how to treat a neighbor, and what the proper ways of engaging in warfare are. The list is exhaustive. An aspect that is also overlooked is one wherein the religious system sets the core foundation of leadership patterns. Recall the prophets: each of them possessed qualities that can be found in modern forms of leadership. Some were gifted listeners with charismatic personalities. Others were able to adapt to changing circumstances in times of need.

They all followed the notion of doing what was in the interests of their people. Those subsequent kings and leaders who played a role in spreading spiritual practices further were often known for their mercy as well as for being just and fair in their dealings. These people gave others purpose and a sense of direction during times when so much of what we currently take for granted was limited. In current times it has become imperative to bring some aspects of religion to our lives, considering how it affects leadership patterns and sets up ethics for people to follow.

Religion affects leadership patterns in ways that sometimes can be easily missed. Rather than diving deep into the complexity of the matter, some religious leaders prefer to keep things simple. City mayors tend to keep a cross in their office just to remind themselves to stay humble.

CEOs rely on apps to remember to pause, repose and pray during hectic working hours in such a fast-paced world. It helped them to stop for a moment and question if they were doing things morally or letting greed get the better of them.

Dr. Moses Haregewoyn

One CEO placed a stone on her office desk, which prompted her to remember the woman taken in adultery and Jesus' intervention.

For her, this was a physical reminder that it's not just her employees who made mistakes, but she could too. It is not necessary that modern religious leaders rely on such tools or symbols. Yet, faith fundamentally impacts leadership principles, practices, and processes. The belief in God can encourage leaders to be servants to both God and their people, which establishes the ethic of strong faith in service. Believing in the Hereafter gives an 'extraordinary' purpose beyond the general finite boundaries of the world: a leader aspiring towards something transcendental, other-worldly, and eternal that offers a sense of responsibility and calmness.

Sacred scriptures serve as an anchor that provides guidance in rapidly changing times and sets the ethical core of guiding and leading others.

Having faith helps bring a sense of relief to a person. Since modern generations are infused with problems of high anxiety, stress, and depression, having a belief in a higher power helps bring some ease. This applies to leaders as well because they shoulder great responsibility, and faith can help make things easier for them, and that, in turn, molds their leadership style and

86

the ethical behaviors they implement in the process. If the belief in a higher power is present, leaders 'may' take things more seriously, and this could strengthen their work ethic overall. In putting the services of others first, they create an atmosphere that encourages the development of trust and allows unity to take form. So as mistakes arise - rather than being too harsh and authoritative, avenues to be more forgiving can be taken to give the person a chance to right their wrongs.

Human beings tend to be drawn to a deeper meaning, and in today's world, since we are so occupied with countless distractions, we yearn for more. Religious systems help provide that, and by giving us baseline norms and values, we have the chance to become more disciplined and find contentment in the simple things.

Leaders are required to keep their people together and safe. They do so by establishing a code of conduct, and their faith helps to inform this. At a collective level, religious leaders should feel *particularly* morally obliged to care about all stakeholders and advocate for sustainable behavior and solutions. They lead not with force but by maintaining good relationships. Providing values is a common theme in leadership through religious systems. Values are not static; they evolve in reflection and produce tradeoffs as well as struggles.

A spiritual structure provides a space to contemplate core values. This is essential to the common moral purpose of spiritual, authentic, and transformational leadership. Religious systems, as well, instill a sense of integrity. An employee will be more likely to refrain from lying and misleading their clients if they have a strong sense of faith.

Leaders tend to surround themselves with like-minded people of similar status. Contemporary leaders are often criticized for keeping to themselves and being out of touch with problems. Such a social bubble can create arrogance and causes leaders to drift from the ground realities. Religious systems, with their attendant ethics, can provide counter spaces to combat this divergence. People are present in a small space where everyone is treated as an equal.

Faith will always play a role in how leadership patterns and styles are formed. Christians use their religious beliefs and practices to model, encourage, enable, inspire and challenge. Leadership models within the varied sects of Christianity span from democratic, servant, transformational, and charismatic to strategic systems. Autocratic leadership was displayed by the actions of King Solomon and King David.

They exercised total authority bestowed upon them by the people. In those harsh, difficult times, the two set a precedent on how to handle matters by implementing all powers bestowed upon them. Democratic leadership was also displayed in Christianity, as well as in the religion of Islam. Islamic democracy holds that people are to elect their leaders. 'Sharia,' the Islamic law, commits to practicing consultation. The Holy Prophet himself would convene with his close advisors in times of need. Jesus Christ displayed servant leadership through the gesture of washing his follower's feet. This kindness displayed how he put the care of others before himself. Charismatic leadership was displayed by individuals such as Martin Luther King. His way of words and dynamic personality played a tremendous role in pushing the Civil Rights movement ahead. Political leaders in Kenya use Pentecostal and Charismatic messaging to stimulate citizens to participate in political activities. Raila Odinga has evoked Biblical charisma in his campaigns for the presidential seat in Kenya for many years.

Strategic leadership was displayed by Moses when he challenged the pharaoh, demanding the release of his people. It was something reminiscent of the David and Goliath story, as one man carried absolute authority while the other was a simple shepherd. Moses was well aware of his limits, so his approach was timed and planned. He did not act impulsively. Religion asserts itself in the aspect of ethics among leaders. This is reflected when leaders dictate to their followers how to behave in organizations on the basis of religious persuasions or non-persuasions. Those who exhibit spiritual tendencies are more likely to detect an ethical problem facing an organization as opposed to leaders who lack a religious background.

Chapter Five - Changes in Organizational Behavior

If there is one thing that all leaders must remember, it is that change is inevitable. Many refuse to accept this because they want to hold on to power or have become too comfortable in their own pattern. This makes them rigid and closed to any forthcoming change. Those who are able to adapt tend to survive. The shift, however, needs to be done properly; otherwise, the changes being made can prove problematic.

If the shift towards something new is not properly done, it can lead to issues with correlated organizational behavior. To understand how the behavior is affected, let us first understand what organizational change is and whether it needs to be done.

Organizational change is the movement of an organization from one state of affairs to another. This can take many forms but mostly centers on structures, policies, procedures, technology, and culture. The change can either be forced due to unexpected circumstances or be planned over a long period of time.

Organizational changes tend to be radical in nature which in turn alters the whole culture and behavior of the employees. If it is done in a slow and steady manner, then the employees may be more prone to adapting. The changes involve letting go of the old ways in which work was done and, instead, adjusting to the new methods.

These changes to the system are due to the following:

- Workforce demographics.

- Technology.

- Globalization.

- Market Conditions.

- Organizational Growth.

- Poor Performance.

Workforce Demographics

Organizations tend to change as a reaction to the shifting environment. This can be due to a rise in the age of the workforce and how that will affect companies in their hiring process and fitting them into their working culture.

Leadership: An Incumbent of Faith

Companies will have to acknowledge the need for appropriate benefits for an aging workforce, and the types of benefits they would want may and/or will change.

Sometimes working hours and job sharing may become more prevalent as employees remain in the workforce, even after retirement.

As the workforce gets older, it may be possible that the employees become bored or unhappy with the nature of their work, which could lead to a large turnover rate.

Management will have to figure out a means to keep these workers motivated and dedicated to their jobs in order to retain them.

Technology

In the last thirty years, technology has become a part of our daily lives in ways that many companies did not expect.

Currently, it is expected that every employee will be provided a computer to work, but there was a time when people were working with pens and paper. With the introduction of computers, workers found themselves having to figure out how to operate their systems. Today, persistent change seems inherent to any given field of technology, and companies have to find ways to keep their employees updated with the latest tech and, most importantly, how to navigate it.

Sometimes technological advances can be difficult to adapt to. An example of this would be the music industry. In the 1980s, CDs were introduced, which were easier and more efficient to handle in comparison to the traditional LPs. This was quite profitable for many record-producing companies as CDs were easier to make, saving on costs and doubling the prices, which brought tremendous profit.

However, these benefits came under threat from the evolution of the internet, when software sharing grew, leading to the development of websites such as Napster and Kazaa. Here people could download music for free, creating an issue for record companies.

Since a change like this hadn't happened before, record companies reacted clumsily by suing all those who participated on these websites, which included underage children. Luckily for them, Apple Inc. addressed the issue and solved it by creating iTunes, which legalized the system of sharing music online.

Globalization

Leadership: An Incumbent of Faith

As the world becomes more interconnected than ever, thanks to the spread of the internet, companies have to adapt to changes at a much faster rate and be open to more cultural matters in order to embrace diversity.

Companies rely on manufacturing from overseas factories since labor abroad is cheaper in comparison to their local settings. Outsourcing has become more common, and now it is important for countries to be more aware of how to make the foreign workforce operate at a desired performance level.

There are occasions when a company realizes that the country from which they're outsourcing follows a radically different work culture, making it imperative that administrators are well informed on the people's work culture and the political climate of their locale. They also have to take into account matters of employee stress due to jobs sent abroad and retraining a workforce on a large scale while competing within a global marketplace.

Market Conditions

The market is known for its history of unpredictability. The world has seen economies thrive but also witnessed their abysmal drops. That's why it's important for companies to adjust to changes depending on market conditions.

Plane tickets used to be expensive prior to the internet, but when online booking became prevalent, companies had to decrease their prices to stay competitive.

However, with the recent rise in oil prices, airline companies have had to readjust pricing to ensure a modicum of loss mitigation.

During the most recent series of economic downturns, certain airlines have merged with others to form a stronger, singular organization with holdings substantial enough to maintain their ongoing viability.

Organizational Growth

All entrepreneurs and leaders want to see their businesses grow. From a small garage store to a large multinational, the leader wants to make their brand and name known.

This is why they need to be willing to embrace changes; otherwise, the company stagnates and is unable to adapt as the size grows larger.

Microsoft and Apple are an example of this. Both companies started with a few young men tinkering with machines in their garages and went on to make the biggest companies in the tech industry.

Leadership: An Incumbent of Faith

Bill Gates and Steve Jobs each had their individual struggles as Microsoft and Apple grew, but despite their stumbles, they managed to bounce back and perform better.

Poor Performance

Sometimes changes occur because the company is not performing at its highest potential. Profits aren't looking bright, and the goals are *far* from being achieved. This requires managers to make an overall change in order to make sure the company gets back on track and performs better.

Those companies that perform poorly are surprisingly more adept at changing than one that is performing well. This is because the latter has achieved a sense of over-confidence and inertia due to their consistent performance over the years.

Since introducing change to a company has been proven beneficial and, on some occasions, necessary, managers find themselves facing off with employees who display resistance.

In fact, resistance to change is a key reason why companies sometimes fail during their transformation. If workers are not on board, it's difficult to get things done. Enthusiastic support is often rare when managers want to bring new things into the system.

There are two forms of resistance, active and passive. Active resistance is, by a degree, the most negative reaction to a proposed series of changes by the management. Employees that participate in active resistance may sabotage the change effort and be vocal about their objections to the new methods.

Passive resistance does not behave in the same manner as extreme resistance, but it does involve being disturbed by the changes being made.

Passive resisters may dislike the changes but not be too vocal about them while displaying signs of stress and sadness. Some of them may secretly seek out jobs elsewhere where they would feel more comfortable.

Then there is the stage of compliance, where the workers go along with the proposed changes with little enthusiasm. They are open to change, but they don't display too much joy about it.

Leadership: An Incumbent of Faith

The most extreme form of cooperation to change is shown in enthusiastic support, where employees are solid proponents of proposed changes encouraging others to join in. If managers wish to bring something new to the table, they will have to first take into account how much support and resistance they will have and to what degree. Those who support the notion will be people the managers can rely on, but this begs the question: why do employees resist these changes even when they know it is for their betterment?

Research states that the following traits lead people to resist changes.

They include:

- Disrupted Habits.

- Personality.

- Uncertainty.

- Fear of Failure.

- Personal Impact of Change.

- Perceived Loss of Power.

Disrupted Habits

As humans, we are slaves to our habits. This is why at times, when someone is made to change, they have a hard time doing so.

Habits become part of our daily routine; hence when it comes to working matters, the resistance to change can be quite strong. If an employee is comfortable working the way they are, they would not like the idea of a 'tactical shift.'

This requires time and effort on everyone's part. With change comes a period of trial and error. This is something no well-established employee wants to experience.

Personality

There are certain people who, by nature, prefer to keep things the way they are. They like the comfort that has been created around them and, to a certain extent, may even thrive in it. When the prospect of change arises, the core aspect of their nature is threatened, and that is why they're hesitant to adapt.

Leadership: An Incumbent of Faith

Those who have a positive self-concept are more capable of adapting than those who do not. This is due to the fact that since they carry high self-esteem, they're more willing to face challenges, whereas those who aren't too sure of themselves prefer to avoid them.

Uncertainty

When something new comes our way, we may be quite unsure of the outcomes and consequences. There can be apprehension regarding moving to a new city or deciding whether to go to a party.

A person may weigh the pros and cons as much as they want, but the dread of uncertainty lingers in their minds.

This happens to employees when they receive news regarding their companies. Suppose a company is choosing to lay off a number of workers; it is evident that an employee not among those being let go will still worry, wondering if their turn is coming next.

This feeling of facing the unknown can cause high stress, which leads to unproductive workplace behavior.

It derives from the core aspect that the employee is losing control of what was once manageable for them.

Fear of Failure

Failure is something that everyone experiences in life and is known to be helpful when one learns from it. Unfortunately, rare are the individuals introspective enough to avoid repetition of personal, not mention learned, mistakes. Despite this, the average individual prefers to avoid stumbling and making errors.

As a result, when management decides to make changes, people resist them because they're concerned they might not be able to adapt; the rate of success they've become accustomed to may be under threat with a new, improved system.

Personal Impact of Change

People are more welcoming to change if they see that it is favorable to them on a personal level. Let's suppose that when managers decide to change working hours while promising a raise or a bonus, their employees may be upset with changes to their schedules and any personal conflicts incurred but will be pleased with their improved salaries.

However, if only hours of work are changed with no benefits for the workers, then they will be more resistant.

Perceived Loss of Power

Sometimes when managements want a redo how the company is run, it creates a point of anxiety for managers as they fear it may affect the power structure at hand. If someone's role and responsibilities are being downgraded, then they are bound to display resistance. In the old structure, supervisors decided who was hired and fired, but in the new systems of today, it's left to the team.

Anyone who was in the supervisor's shoes would not be happy to see that their means of control and influence had been sidelined.

Is Resistance Bad?

The term resistance does not necessarily have a fixed meaning. Some view it as something negative but sometimes saying 'no' isn't always a bad thing. In the context mentioned above, we've seen how resistance tends to cause problems because people are not willing to adapt to the changing times and this, in turn, affects the whole company.

On some occasions, if the managers and the leaders are indeed leading people to more trouble, then resistance might be a good thing.

Dr. Moses Haregewoyn

Managers have a tendency to assume that those who refuse to follow new protocols are simply difficult employees. What they should consider is how resistance to change is, in fact, a valuable feedback tool that should not be ignored.

This leads to an opportunity to understand why the people are not happy with the new policies. Since it's the managers' and leaders' responsibility to understand their workers better, a receptive and introspective approach gives the manager a chance to do so.

By enforcing changes, the company is setting a negative approach that would make the employees seek work elsewhere. Instead, listening to the workers and incorporating their suggestions into the change effort would be more beneficial for both parties.

This can help them come to a mutual understanding. Whenever an employee sees the management willing to give them a listening ear, they make an effort to perform better.

In some companies, there are employees who are strongly committed to the organization, while others are not. The former ones can, at times, be the most resistant to changes.

Their fear stems from the notion that the implemented changes will, in turn, threaten their strong attachment and, with time, hurt the company.

Those with weak loyalty tend to comply with the changes because they have little concern about whether the company will survive.

This contrast highlights for managers that when dealing with those personalities who are strongly resistant to change, it is important now not to question their loyalty for not offering their cooperation.

This blame-game approach would only hurt their loyal sentiments, and their resistance would only increase.

Planning and Executing Change Effectively

Since resistance is bound to happen when a company decides to make changes within the system, the question hangs heavy on the managers' shoulders, 'how can we make changes effectively with less resistance?'

This is where Kurt Lewin's three-stage model of planned change comes in handy.

Dr. Moses Haregewoyn

He established a framework that could help leaders decide on their approach when bringing changes to the company and strategies for balancing management-employee relations.

According to Lewin, there is an automatic assumption that change is bound to bring resistance. Without prior preparation, executing the changes are likely to fail.

Lewin suggested in his framework that an organization should begin with 'unfreezing.' The term here means making sure that members of the company are ready for and receptive to change prior to implementation.

Once unfreezing is completed, 'change' or executing the planned change is initiated.

Since there's already been groundwork done during the unfreezing stage, the resistance factor is comparatively less.

Then comes the final stage of 'refreezing,' which involves ensuring that the new changes are made permanent, which includes new habits, rules, and procedures that are made the norm. This framework does summarize how to go about bringing change, but there is a specificity required to make it work, so let's dive further into Lewin's framework.

106

Leadership: An Incumbent of Faith

In recent times, there has been more coordination between the leader and the worker. The hierarchy has become more inclusive, which allows for two-way dialogue.

The leaders and managers can bring about change by:

- Creating a vision.

- Communicating a plan for change.

- Developing a sense of urgency.

- Building coalitions.

- Providing support.

- Allowing employee participation.

- Establishing small wins.

- Removing obstacles.

- Initiating refreezing.

- Publicizing success.

- Augmenting to the prior changes made.

- Rewarding those who adopt changes.

- Instituting change as a cultural norm in the workplace.

Create a Vision

It's expected that all leaders have the vision to achieve. When it comes to making changes, they need to have an overall picture of their objective. So, to bring a change, the vision needs to be clear, inspiring and motivating in order for others to follow. People will take pride when following a vision they're truly a part of.

Communicate a Plan for Change

Having a plan is not enough. Leaders need to be able to articulate it to their people in a way that is understood and encourages them to join in on the effort. If there is a communication gap, then that can lead to misunderstandings and alienate the workers.

When employees know what's going to happen- the how, the when, and the way it reduces their discomfort. It's generally keeping them in the dark about the changes that lead them to be resistant.

Those who are made fully aware of the necessary information are likely to be committed to making changes.

The act of leaders communicating with their workers does not just boost morale support, but it provides a symbolic value.

Most people work their usual shifts and leave, feeling mostly useless. When a leader makes an effort to talk to them, it strengthens loyalty.

Develop a Sense of Urgency

Accepting change does not come easy when the work environment has reached an equilibrium and the ease of 'routine.' Most people become comfortable and then rigid in their daily activities.

As the recent pandemic has keenly illustrated for all of us, good leadership would then need to maintain an atmosphere that promotes openness to the challenges of change and a sense of urgency to counteract the inevitability of complacency, so employees maintain adaptability.

In times of strife that affect the reputation or the needs of the business, and when flexibility and adaptability have been cultivated amongst employees, a willingness towards accountability and a desire to take the necessary courses of action will prevail to ensure the survival of the business.

Alternately, those employees who have been allowed to languish to the point of recalcitrance with no challenges presented to their routines as normative will lack a sense of urgency and may respond in times of need for maximum contribution in dire forms, including the exodus from the company.

Building Coalitions

When notifying workers of upcoming changes, a leader doesn't necessarily have to explain his agenda to each person individually. People's opinions towards change are, in one way or another, influenced by opinion leaders.

These are workers who have a significant influence on their coworkers' behavior and attitudes due to any number of factors.

They don't have to be someone in a managerial post, necessarily, but an individual who has the social skills and articulations to move others.

Leaders need to identify these opinion leaders and prepare them to pass on the changes.

Once an opinion leader is convinced that the company has to bring reforms, then they will pass the message on and influence those around them.

The opinion leaders will automatically become helping hands and will ensure that the company is ready for change.

Provide Support

It's important that when implementing changes, employees don't feel their needs are being overlooked or ignored. Hence, management needs to provide emotional support when necessary. This can be done through discussion, encouragement, and expressing confidence in an employee's ability to perform effectively under the new system.

Allow Employee Participation

When employees are allowed to participate in planning the changes, they tend to have more of a positive and upbeat attitude toward the change because they have been offered a chance to voice their concerns and opinions. The worker has a better intellectual grasp of why the specific changes are being made, what the alternatives are, and what to expect when the agenda's initiated.

This feeling of ownership drives them to help the leader in making the changes happen and facilitates implementation.

When these steps are done, and leaders now have a strong coalition and level of trust of their workers, they can proceed with implementing the second stage of Lewin's framework, which is executing change.

With this, the company witnesses different changes in technology, structure, culture, and procedure. This can lead to employees experiencing high amounts of stress. Even if they were informed, there is still a bit of difficulty during the first few days. It is one thing to discuss and another to experience. Mistakes become frequent, and there is uncertainty present regarding people's jobs.

It is now up to management to make sure that the stress levels do not hit an all-time high. They must display support and patience and continue giving support when needed until the changes are complete.

Encourage Small Wins

During the changing period, management needs to make the workers feel that despite the mistakes being made, they are still doing well in other ways. This can be done by making a history of small wins. It will show the workers that change is a step-by-step process, and slowly they are getting closer to their goal.

If the change is large in scope and the results won't show in the short term, then employees may lose sight of their accomplishments.

If the workers see the changes and improvements, they will be motivated to do better. This is why it is important to break the proposed changes into phases that will balance the time to witness the little successes. Having small targets will keep the workers going, and they will know that they have the capability to continue further.

Eliminate Obstacles

During the changing period, it is common for obstacles to arise. This can come in the form of people who at first supported the changes but are now undermining them. Sometimes the obstacles appear within a structure, process, or culture as well. It's up to managers to identify and understand how these problems can be effectively dealt with.

With these steps implemented, the company is now witnessing a considerable shift from the old ways and transitioning into something new. At this point, leaders assist their workers in acclimating so that new habits and procedures become the norm. The refreezing step(s) needs to be taken during that time.

Publicize Success

To make the changes permanent, sharing the results is important. The employees will see firsthand how the new elements are beneficial, and now, to make the work easier, the changes are to be made the norm.

Leaders need to highlight what were the things that benefitted the company and credit the workers for making it possible.

Add on to the Prior Changes Made

When the results start becoming evident, leaders need to take that chance to implement more changes because the company's gained ongoing momentum.

This will establish continuous improvement, doubling the results once the changes are inaugurated.

Rather than declaring success early, leaders should take a step back in order to observe both the major shifts and the finer nuances these continuous improvements have made and whether they're working in the right order.

Rewards Those Who Adopt Changes

Making permanent changes is never easy, but it can be done by rewarding those who embrace these changes. Those individuals who sign on, who understand and share a unifying vision, can serve as an example for others to follow. The rewards do not have to be financial.

The act of giving recognition to those who have adapted to change well in front of others is a source of motivation for many, and they will be more willing to let the changes become the norm.

When new behaviors are made a part of an organization's reward system, those behaviors are taken more seriously and repeated by others.

Make Change a Norm in the Workplace Culture

Dr. Moses Haregewoyn

If the change is successful, it will become part of the corporate culture.

All the additions made in procedures, processes, or technology will become instilled in the mindset of the workers. What was once difficult to adapt to is now a part of everyday life.

Chapter Six - Leadership Skills, Traits, and Behaviors

'Leadership' is something of an umbrella term in today's world. However, the central defining concept revolves around leading others.

Many unique individuals across history have displayed their different styles of guiding others, but as of today, due to the many different types of leadership models we have, it can be a bit tricky to categorize them.

One distinction that separates leadership concepts is between leadership skills and behavior.

To understand how they differentiate from one another, it's better to have an understanding of both concepts.

Leadership skills are the competencies and knowledge that a leader possesses and uses to successfully reach goals and objectives.

Effective leadership is determined by three types of personal skills which are:

- Technical skills.

- Interpersonal skills.

- Conceptual skills.

Technical Skills

Technical skills include knowledge about an organization's work, structure, and rules. Also, proficiency in specialized activities and an understanding the methods, processes, and equipment used by organizational units are necessary.

Technical skills may be acquired through various means, including formal education, on-the-job training, and experience. Technical skills are essential for supervisory and middle management leaders but somewhat less important for senior leaders and those in top management.

Interpersonal or Human Skills

Whereas technical skills involve working with things, interpersonal or human skills are all about working with people. Leaders should have knowledge of human behavior and group processes, and they should be able to understand the feelings, attitudes, and motives of their followers.

Interpersonal skills enable public health leaders to work cooperatively with subordinates, peers, and superiors, as

Leadership: An Incumbent of Faith

well as with constituents and collaborators. One crucial component of the interpersonal skill set is empathy. Empathy is the capacity to understand other people's values, motives, and emotions. Empathy also involves social insight to determine what behaviors are acceptable in particular situations.

The ability to select an appropriate influence strategy as a leader depends on knowing what followers want and how followers perceive a situation. Leaders who continuously monitor themselves better understand their behavior and how it impacts their followers. Such leaders can adjust their behavior to match specific conditions.

Other interpersonal skills useful in the leadership influence process include oral communication ability and persuasiveness.

Effective leadership is fundamentally based on interpersonal competence. Leaders with strong interpersonal skills enhance group cooperation, support the pursuit of common goals, and have success with influence and impression management tactics. Fundamental skills in working with others need to be practiced and demonstrated on a daily basis. Since the nature of compassionate leadership involves sensitivity during decision-making and in the day-to-day behavior of the individual, it has to become a natural, continuous activity.

Everything a leader says and does have an effect on his or her associates. In order to be effective, skills need to be developed naturally and unconsciously, as well as consistently.

For public health leaders, interpersonal or human skills can be summarized simply as the ability to get along with followers as they do their work. Such skills are important at all levels, from supervisors and middle management to the organization's top management positions.

Conceptual Skills

Just as technical skills involve working with things and interpersonal skills include working with people, conceptual skills involve working with ideas and concepts. Conceptual skills incorporate a variety of attributes, including judgment, intuition, creativity, and foresight.

Some conceptual skills, such as inductive or deductive reasoning, logical thinking, analytical ability, and concept formation- can be measured using aptitude tests.

Leadership: An Incumbent of Faith

Effective strategic planning is a key responsibility for shaping any organization's or movement's future, especially during difficult times. It requires that leaders have the ability to prognostic based on current trends.

Additionally, intuition is of tremendous importance because it develops in the leaders' repertoire through experience with certain types of problems.

Effective leaders often blend conscious reasoning with intuition, depending on the situation.

Conceptual skills are the most important skill set for senior public health leaders and upper-level managers. Senior leaders can put the entire organization, or their people, without strong conceptual skills, at risk.

Leadership Traits

Every leader has a series of traits that make them stand out from the crowd. Whenever there is a person who seems to lead, even invigorate, a conversation or has a natural talent for getting people to follow them. It's because they have the necessary qualities to galvanize and organize others.

In order to possess leadership qualities, there are traits one must have, which are:

- Intelligence.

- Self-Confidence and Determination.

- Personal Integrity.

Intelligence

Intelligence, or intellectual or cognitive ability, includes the mental capacity for understanding, reasoning, and clarity of perception. They must possess the aptitude for grasping facts and the ability to identify any relationships between them.

Although not every leader needs to be gifted with high intelligence, it is still an important trait required to lead others. A leader can become impeded if their intellectual ability differs significantly from that of their followers. Effective leaders must be able to explain complex concepts in a manner that meets the needs of their followers.

Self-Confidence and Determination

Leaders with self-confidence have realistic certainties in their judgment, ideas, ability, power, decision-making, and skills. Such leaders know and trust themselves without pride or arrogance. They have a positive attitude about themselves and are able to press ahead with the belief that, if and when they make a wrong decision, any setback can be overcome.

Effective leaders have self-assurance and self-esteem. They understand that their leadership can and will make a difference to their organization and that their influence on others is suitable and appropriate.

Determination is the motivation a leader needs to come to a decision, and it includes characteristics such as energy, initiative, persistence, and tenacity. Leaders with determination have the perseverance required to see a job through to completion and to persevere in the face of obstacles.

Personal Integrity

Personal integrity- the adherence to personal values in day-to-day behavior- is a predominant aspect of interpersonal trust. Effective leaders show their character by being ethical, trustworthy, and honest. Concerning integrity, leaders must 'walk the talk.'

Integrity is foundational in relationships between leaders and followers. Leaders who demonstrate integrity receive admiration, respect, and loyalty from followers.

Dr. Moses Haregewoyn

However, if leaders are not deemed trustworthy, they receive no loyalty from followers, and relationships between peers and superiors will be impossible to maintain.

Being of service to followers and recognizing that loyalty is a two-way street both signal a high level of leadership integrity. Effective leaders live by the same rules they establish for followers; to do otherwise violates their followers' trust.

Lies and deceit with followers result in a loss of friendship and/or credibility. Exploitation, manipulation, and failure to keep promises likewise compromise a leader's effectiveness. Leaders who act in their own self-interest lose the trust of their followers. If leaders fail to maintain followers' confidence, effective communication and the flow of useful information become hampered.

Leaders refusing to take responsibility for their actions and decisions are perceived as undependable or worse, especially if they try to blame others for their failures. When a breach of personal integrity becomes obvious, effective leadership ceases.

Chapter Seven - Weak Leadership

We're familiar now with the importance of strong leadership and its positive effects on the sole leader and those surrounding him or her. However, knowing one side of the coin is not enough. If we are to truly have a better understanding of how leadership works, then we need to take into account how weak leadership can be a problem and how it can cause tremendous harm.

There is a lot of pressure on the sole leader to do things correctly, and they're expected to take the blame when things fall apart. A genuine leader will accept responsibility, while a bad one will scapegoat the team. Sometimes the situation isn't always so black and white.

Leaders can try their best and still fall short of expectations. Sometimes they are not cut out for the task at hand. Let's take a deeper dive into understanding how weak leadership is displayed and how that affects the followers.

The fact that poor-quality leadership has negative effects on individuals is nothing new. Throughout history, megalomaniacs take control and lead their people to destruction, such as Hitler, Pol Pot, and Osama Bin Laden. Upon attaining their possessions of leadership and totalitarian authority, they put the lives and interests of their people at stake. Rather than guiding them in a better direction, they let their egos, with unbridled hatred and biases, destroy everything.

Weak leadership not only affects the circumstances but also has a negative effect on people's mental health as well. Poor leadership has been associated with high levels of employee stress and retaliation. Whenever abusive supervisors used non-contingent punishments, employees and followers, felt a sense of helplessness, dread, and alienation from their work.

In the military, the leadership effectiveness of commanding officers is negatively affected when they resort to non-contingent punishment. Soldiers experience high levels of psychological distress when under such authority.

Administrators lacking the appropriate skill sets may be abusive, aggressive, or punitive. Employees, in general, who perceive their supervisors to be offensive, experience low levels of job and life satisfaction, low levels of affective commitment, increased work-family conflict, and psychological distress, which include symptoms of anxiety and depression.

Abusive Leadership

Abusive leadership occurs when individuals in a formal leadership role engage in aggressive or punitive behaviors toward their employees. These behaviors range from bosses degrading their employees by yelling, ridiculing, or name-calling.

Abuse can take the form of a boss terrorizing employees through withholding information or threatening them with job loss and pay cuts. These tactics are considered workplace harassment, emotional abuse, or simply workplace aggression. The impact of such behaviors is exaggerated by the position of the perpetrator. Aggressive acts by supervisors may have more deleterious effects on employee outcomes than similar acts committed by members of the public or other coworkers.

Passive Leadership

Sometimes being aggressive isn't necessarily the reason behind poor leadership skills. There are occasions when a leader lacks the necessary social dexterity/acumen to guide others, be it a lack of vision, charm, or an overarching aversion to risk-taking.

Leaders who participate in this passive nature do not intervene until problems are brought to their attention or become severe enough to demand action. They tend to avoid decision-making and the responsibilities that are handed to them.

Lack of Vision

Vision is an important ingredient for leaders. It's a future-oriented mindset, which focuses on the bigger picture. Those visionary leaders can clearly envision the action required for their team to reach their organization's goals. Vision is something of a road map that people rely on, and it can only be created, set, and articulated by a strong leader. By not having a view of the gestalt, people can feel adrift and unsure of what they should be doing.

Vision isn't something strictly placed in writing; it needs to be demonstrated. If it doesn't come from a genuine belief and lacks heart, it lacks the weight and vision required to motivate others.

Poor Communication Skills

Leadership: An Incumbent of Faith

Leadership requires a robust set of communication skills. The stronger the ability to articulate, the better employees understand, thereby strengthening their beliefs. Effective communication helps people and inspires them to follow the principles and values which are displayed by the leader. Without clear communication, leadership cannot exist.

If this component's weak, the outcomes are less than desirable.

The main reason communication is important is its interdependence on vision. One cannot function without the other. Anyone can have an idea of where they want to go, but without putting it into words, not many will be willing to traverse the same journey.

Poor communication even weakens and sabotages relationships within an organization. If people do not feel heard or communicate ineffectively, then it is only a matter of time before people start leaving altogether.

Lack of Management Skill

Leaders need to share the qualities of managers. There is a necessity for both management and leadership skills to be set in equal frequency. Management functions include planning, organizing, execution, and control, but to execute them, management skills are needed. These include skills that are technical, social, and conceptual.

When these traits are lacking in a supervisor, employees have placed faith in someone who isn't up to the tasks and challenges of management. This weakens trust and confidence and, in the process, loyalty to the team founders.

Everyone tends to become individualistic or collective in nature, and this can undermine the spirit of teamwork because if people are not united for a common cause, it's challenging to reach the intended goals. This is why a leader must ensure they display managerial skills among the other crucial leadership qualities.

Personal attention given to employees by the boss goes a long way in establishing a viable connection; workers feel seen, thus, are inspired to do better.

Poor Example Setting

One of the most important and influential ways leaders influence others is by setting an example for others to follow. Leaders do this in order to have their followers emulate the same actions, i.e., follow in their footsteps. A brilliant mind,

Leadership: An Incumbent of Faith

Albert Einstein, once said, "setting an example is not a major way of influencing others. Rather it is the only way."

Leaders are automatically identified by others. This puts them in an elevated position where they are prone to both praise and criticism. If they set the standard on how to behave ethically, then others will follow them because they are an inspirational example.

If the leader does not, however, set an example, people won't be interested in following them. In fact, some might adopt the negative traits being displayed.

Leaders should live exemplary life that brings positive impact. They have to walk the talk, meaning they must display consistency between the words and deeds of the leader. The statement 'actions speak louder than words' applies strongly to this concept. Anyone can rise and talk big, but the exceptions are the ones who show results and take the initiative.

Nowadays, empty words are tossed about, and very little is done. Anyone can post an angry rant on social media about any given injustice, but they don't set foot on the streets and fight against the unjust systems. If anyone chooses to actually make an effort to change things, then automatically, like a moth to the flame, people will start to follow. Sometimes all they need is a little hope.

Poor Motivational Skill

Motivation is necessary for a leader to guide their people. It helps bring individuals together and gives them the spirit of being consistent in achieving their goals. There are two types of motivation, intrinsic and extrinsic. The former refers to motivation from within, whereas the latter means motivation coming from an external source.

Suppose the leader is motivated from within, then they are capable of leading their cause. However, if their drive is flawed, then it will start to show, which automatically may turn their followers away.

Extrinsic motivation occurs when we observe someone participate in a behavior that inspires us to follow. If workers see how much hard work and hope the leader puts in, they will provide better output in exchange.

If a leader fails to motivate themselves, then they cannot push others to do the same.

Effects of Poor Leadership

Leadership: An Incumbent of Faith

The negativity caused by weak leadership creates a poor culture in the workplace. Where morale is low, mediocrity starts to grow. No one is inspired to try new ideas and take risks, so instead, workers follow a 'clock in, clock out' approach to their jobs. Productivity declines in the process, and this costs the company as a whole.

Turnover rates grow when workers feel undervalued or have little faith in management's ability to make things better, and that's when they start job hunting. Losing workers only escalate problems and responsibilities.

Targeted goals are never reached, and support for obtaining them lessens. You end up getting an organization where people do as they are told with little inspiration or motivation.

Chapter Eight - Why Understanding Leadership is Tricky

We know what leadership is by definition, and although there are different styles of it, there are times when it can be challenging to analyze. This is because many of those researching it tend to misconceive their tasks. It is common for researchers to look more into popularity, power, showmanship, or wisdom in long-term planning. These are contributing factors to leadership, but they do not define it as a whole. They are merely traits and not the essence.

Leadership is the accomplishment of a goal through the direction of human assistants. You will see figures who can get people on their side and use their skills to help accomplish a needed goal. A great leader is one who can do this daily and consistently regardless of the changing circumstances that come their way. Whoever successfully manages to do so is considered a good leader.

This distinction is important because there have been examples where leaders have been good for a particular time

134

Leadership: An Incumbent of Faith

but did not do so well when the circumstances changed. An example of this is Winston Churchill. The Prime Minister was a good leader in times of war, but when he was re-elected in 1951, he only served one term, and many critics feel it wasn't his best tenure. There is a separation between leaders who are good during times of crisis and those who are needed in times of peace. A great leader would be one that can manage both circumstances and reliably succeed in achieving his or her goal.

This leader may not necessarily possess or display power; force or the threat of harm may never enter into their dealings. He might not even be popular among the people or have a colorful, charismatic personality. Yet, despite these setbacks, he is still able to carry out the plans of others.

You may wonder how someone with no charm, personality, or likable skills can be good at handling both situations? There is the example of Canadian Prime Minister Mackenzie King. King served as the tenth Prime Minister of Canada for three non-consecutive terms from 1921-1926, 1926-1930, and 1935-1948. He led his nation from the chaos caused by the Great Depression and successfully managed to help the allies defeat the Axis powers in World War II. He was present even during peacetime and helped his country transition from a colonial state to an independent nation. These accomplishments have set quite the precedent for good leadership. Now comes a twist, Mackenzie King was by no means a charming or powerful personality. Surrounded by the prominent personalities of Churchill, Roosevelt, and De Gaulle, a King, was deemed to be quite dull and tactless in human relations. He lacked oratorical skills, and his personality did not resonate with the electorate. King wasn't even married and did not have a charming wife who could perhaps compensate for his dull nature.

Now how can a man with all these traits manage to accomplish so much for the country? This goes to show that you don't need generic popularity and charm to be a great leader; you simply need to know how to get the job done. What King lacked in charisma, he made up for in his policies and their implementation.

However, most researchers tend to overlook him because they do not see any mention of a rabble-rousing demagogue with whom much associates leadership. They do not understand that a leader's unique achievement is a human and a social one that stems from an understanding of his fellow workers and the relationships of their individual goals to the group goal that he must carry out.

Clement Atlee is another example of this. When World War 2 ended, many would expect that Churchill was bound to win another election due to his success in the war, yet the people chose someone who was a complete contradiction to him. Clement Atlee lacked personality and charm, and yet he managed to bring the Labor party to the forefront of England's politics, leading them through a time of recovery and healing. Despite his lack of oratory skills and charm, people still regarded him as a good leader who was needed at that time.

Flaws and Delusions

It is easy to say that what successful leaders do makes them effective in just a few words. However, it is more challenging to figure out the specific components determining their success. The usual method is for the leader to provide recognition of each worker's requirements so that that individual can foresee the satisfaction of some primary goal's fruition as a result of their role in the group enterprise.

The usual forms of leadership tend to focus on sources of satisfaction, e.g., money or assurances of comfortable security. People work and follow their leader because they know that getting the work done will get them paid. If they refuse, they will be fired.

This approach to motivating others is effective but only for a limited time- period. There will come the point where people want something more than simply churning out work day after day. This is where the leader's personality comes into play by authentically making his followers feel important. Humans aren't machines that can be activated with the push of a button.

Every human being has internal complexities that, for a perceptive leader, can really inform a strategy for managing them effectively. People look at aspects of love, prestige, independence, achievement, and feeling a sense of belonging as well to keep themselves motivated.

Here lies a bit of irony; when we think of great leaders, it's common for many to point to historical military leaders. Yet, we just mentioned that people are not machines functioning in a fixated state. So why do we choose military men as good leaders when most of their followers have an intuitive approach to work?

Leadership: An Incumbent of Faith

One explanation for this is that military organizations are the closest thing to a pure example wherein the traditional and ultimately unimaginative application of the simple reward and punishment paradigm is used as a motivator. This doesn't necessarily mean that the military is wrong. It has its own mechanism and serves a definite and clear purpose.

Two observations that are relevant to defending the military are:

It has special problems because, in their battle scenarios, the stakes are too high for a trial-and-error approach. Mistakes and lousy decision-making can lead to men dying. There is a never-ending need for fulfillment and replacement in wartime ranks. Like standard and interchangeable parts, all soldiers are appendages of a more enormous beast that must function efficiently and automatically. This is why the training and treatment of the soldier are, by and large, one of uniformity and mechanization.

Clarity is present about duties and responsibilities due to the autocratic chain of command. This is essential in warfare.

In any given situation, be it at work or a casual meeting among friends, there is someone who has to be the boss. In the latter, the dynamics show themselves. Yet, it is problematic to confuse an organization's chain of command or table as a method of getting things done.

Relations with People

When a leader succeeds. It is usually because they have learned two basic lessons:

- People are complex- not black and white.

- Everyone is different.

Humans are driven by various needs and external factors. Internal, highly personal motivators that a leader keys in on include ambition, patriotism, love of the good and the beautiful, and even boredom or self-doubt. Also, when it comes to labor, humans respond to these internal and external motivators, which take varied forms, e.g., the traditional carrot and stick.

Dimensions and patterns of thought and feeling are as unique as our fingerprints, yet our unifying needs abound at a basic level. In other words, the strength and importance of specific interests aren't the same for every worker, nor is the degree to which they experience job satisfaction.

Here are some other examples:

- One person may be characterized primarily by a deep religious need but find that fact irrelevant to daily work.

- Others may find their utmost satisfaction in solving philosophical problems and never be led to discover how their love for chess problems and mathematical puzzles can be applied to their business.

- Or still, another may need an admiring relationship that they lack at home and be constantly frustrated by the failure of their superior to recognize and take advantage of that need.

- To the extent that the leader's circumstances and skill permit them to respond to such individual patterns, they'll be better able to create genuinely intrinsic interest in the work that they're charged with getting done.

Limits of the Golden Rule

Fortunately, the prime motives of people living in the same culture are often very similar, and some general motivational rules work very well indeed. The famous statement 'treat others as you would like to be treated' is a variation of the golden rule. While limited and oversimplified, such a rule dramatically improves over the primitive coercive approaches or the straight reward-for-desired-behavior approach.

It would be wrong not to recognize that some of the world's most ineffective leadership comes from the 'treat others as you would be treated' school.

All of us have known selfless people who earnestly wished to satisfy their fellow humans' needs but were nevertheless entirely socially inept as executives because it never occurred to them that others had tastes or emotional requirements different from their own.

We all know the tireless worker who recognizes no one else's fatigue or boredom, the barroom-story addict who thinks it's jolly to regale even the ladies with his favorite anecdotes, the devotee of public service who tries to win friends and influence people by offering them tickets to lectures on missionary work in Africa, the miserly man who thinks everyone is after money, and many more. Leadership requires more subtlety and perceptiveness than is implied in the saying, 'do as you would be done by.'

Leadership: An Incumbent of Faith

The one who leads us effectively must seem to understand our goals and purposes as well as the implications of his own actions and be able to satisfy them respectively. He must appear to be consistent and clear in his decisions.

The word 'seem' is important here. If we do not apprehend the would-be leader as one who has these traits, it will make no difference how able he may really be. We will still not follow his lead. If, on the other hand, we have been fooled and he merely seems to have these qualities, we still follow him until we discover our error. In other words, the impression he makes at any one time will determine his influence on his followers.

Pitfalls of Perception

For followers to recognize their leader completely, as he really is, may be as tricky as it is for them to understand his followers to the same degree. Some of the worst difficulties in relationships between superiors and subordinates come from misperceiving reality. So much of what we understand in the world around us is colored by the conceptions and prejudices we hold.

The view of the employer or 'superior' may be so blurred by expectations based on the behavior of other bosses that facts may not be interpreted in the same way for each of the players involved. Many failures of leadership can be traced to oversimplified misperceptions on the part of the worker or to failures of the superior to recognize the context or frame within which their actions will be understood by the subordinate.

Look at it another way; imagine an individual who's warm, intelligent, ambitious, and thoughtful. You more than likely have conjured some image of this in your mind. However, if I describe another person as cold, ambitious, thoughtful, and intelligent, then the idea summoned is quite different. This has occurred by simply changing one word and the order of others. The kind of preparation that one adjective gives for those that follow is tremendously effective in determining what meaning will be given to them.

The term 'thoughtful' may mean thoughtful of others or perhaps rational when it is applied to a warm person towards whom we have already accepted a positive orientation, but as used to a cold man, the same term may mean brooding, calculating, and plotting. We must learn to be aware of the degree to which one set of observations about a man may lead us to erroneous conclusions about his other behavior.

Leadership: An Incumbent of Faith

Imagine showing two groups of test subjects a recorded exchange between an employer and his subordinate. The scene portrays disagreement, followed by anger and dismissal.

The blame for the difficulty will be assigned very differently by the two groups if I have shown one a scene of the worker earlier in a happy, loving family breakfast setting, while the other group has seen instead a breakfast table scene where the worker snarls at his family and storms out of the house. The altercation will be understood altogether differently by people who have had favorable or unfavorable, or unfavorable glimpses of the character in question.

In a workplace, a worker may perceive an offer of increased authority as a dangerous removal from the safety-assured, though gradual, promotion. A change in channels of authority or reporting, no matter how valuable in increasing efficiency, may be thought of as a personal challenge or affront.

The introduction of a labor-saving process may be perceived as a threat to one's job. An invitation to discuss company policy may be perceived as an elaborate trap to entice one into admitting heretical or disloyal views. A new fringe benefit may be regarded as an excuse not to pay higher salaries and so on.

Too often, the superior is entirely unprepared for these interpretations, and they seem to him foolish, dishonest, or perverse- all three, but the successful leader will have been prepared for such responses. He will have known that many of his workers have been brought up to consider their employers as their natural enemies, and that habit has made it second nature for them to 'act like an employee' in this respect and always to be suspicious of otherwise friendly overtures from above.

The other side of the same situation is as bad. The habit of acting like a boss can be destructive, too. For example, much resistance to modern concepts of industrial relations comes from employers who think such ideas pose too great a threat to the long-established picture of themselves as business autocrats. Their image makes progress in labor relations difficult.

Troubles of a Subordinate

Another subtle factor may intervene between employer and employee- a factor that will be recognized and dealt with by successful industrial leaders. That factor is the psychological difficulty of being a subordinate. It is not easy to be a subordinate. If someone takes orders from another, it limits the scope of my independent decision and judgment; certain areas are established within which I do what he wishes instead of what I wish.

To accept such a role without friction or rebellion, I must find in it a reflection of some form of order that goes beyond my own personal situation (I.e., age, class, rank, etc.) 32or perhaps find that the balance of dependence and independence actually suits my needs. These two possibilities lead to different practical consequences.

Firstly, it is harder to take orders from one whom I do not consider in some sense superior. One of the saddest failures in practical leadership may indeed be the executive who tries so hard to be one of the boys that he destroys any vestige of awe that his workers might have had for him, with the consequence that they begin to see him as a man like themselves and to wonder why they should take orders from him.

An understanding leader will not let his workers think that he considers them inferior, but he may be wise to maintain a kind of psychological distance that permits them to accept his authority without resentment.

When you have two individuals, and one has more superiority than the other and needs to make decisions, he won't be able to avoid frustrating the subordinate every now and then by interfering in their goals. Frustration tends to lead to aggression, hence creating conflict. In the process, a lot of thwarting brings out the natural tendency to fight back. Once this becomes a habit, both subordinate and superior are bound to have shouting matches.

The situation can worsen for the organization if the employees feel it is not right to let their anger out at their boss, but in the act of staying silent, the frustration grows further, creating a vicious cycle. Anyone can place suggestion boxes, grievances committees, departmental rivalries, and other such gestures may help temporarily, as it helps provide some form of catharsis, but in the long run, an effective leader must be aware of the need to balance dependence with independence, constraint with autonomy, so that taking orders does not feel too big a responsibility.

An effective leader will acknowledge that most people are frightened by complete independence, and they need a sense of security that places certain limits on their freedom. He will make an effort to readjust the levels and kinds of freedom to give depending on the subordinate's psychological needs. This involves providing a developmental program in which the employee can be given some sense of where he is going within the company, and the effective leader will make sure that the view is a realistic one.

There is no point in pretending to give responsibility in decision-making to subordinates when it doesn't exist. To make dependency tolerable, the lines must be clearly drawn between those decisions that are the prerogative of the superior and those that can be caused by or in consultation with the subordinate. Once those lines have been drawn, it is essential not to transgress them any more often than is absolutely necessary.

Ideally, the subordinate should have an area within which they are free to operate without anyone looking over their shoulder.

The superior should clarify the goals and perhaps suggest alternative ways of achieving them, but the subordinate should feel free to make the necessary choices.

This may not go well with those who identify as autocratic leaders.

If the subordinate knows that the boss likes plan A, he isn't going to risk trying plan B and risk his job in case the attempt fails.

When he learns that his job rides on every major decision, he can only play safe by aligning himself in every case with his superior's views, but that doesn't give him freedom.

Instead, what exists is a machine that is doing as it is told, with nothing new being brought to the table. He will have no respect and be treated in a 'do this, do that' manner.

Goals in Development

With every decision that needs to be made, there is always a requirement to balance risk and returns. If outcomes were specific, we wouldn't need someone to make a judgment call.

Making errors is, to a degree, expected. No amount of experience can prevent them from happening. What is expected, though, is that employees learn from them and not repeat them. The executives should keep an eye on the long-term growth of their workers to see if their successes outweigh the losses.

This is important in the long run for growth and for continuing leadership. Each worker needs to know their role in the group and be open to development, even if it's limited.

The workers need to see the leader as a person who is invested in their growth.

Allowing workers to have a say in policymaking isn't enough. Subordinates can help technically, but they shouldn't be overstepping by consulting on matters that are an executive's responsibility.

Dealing on a Personal Level

There can never be any genuine growth of an employee without teaching.

The one in charge needs to take out time and make sure that the subordinate is cognizant of their successes in addition to their blind spots and any consequences that they/the company may experience as a result.

This might be an uncomfortable discussion, but it's necessary. No improvement comes without hurt feelings. It

Dr. Moses Haregewoyn

is primarily the harsh lessons and the big mistakes that teach us the most.

However, when it comes down to having that difficult conversation, it is difficult to do so because a leader needs to contemplate the following:

- How can criticism be impersonal and still effective?

- How can a decision or a method be criticized without the worker feeling that he is personally being demeaned?

When offering adequate coaching or criticism – A leader can risk long-range damage to the employees' morale, but a specific short-range effect is usually often the employee's failure to perform as instructed when carrying out the boss's alternative plan. The failure constitutes proof that the manager was correct in the first place. Without essential communication where positive and negative reinforcement occurs, it is easy for a leader to create antagonism and defensiveness by dealing impersonally with a problem and forgetting the human emotions and motives that are involved in it.

These situations tend to occur mostly in the office than anywhere else. This is why it is important to learn how to get along with others as soon as possible. In the long run, being the rebel or the disliked person in the room never helps. It's almost second nature to create a personal and emotional setting that is right for a particular person in the household, which ought to be the same approach in a working environment.

"Low-Pressure" Leadership

In most workplaces, there are many executives who aren't necessarily authentic. They simply mimic the surface characteristics of some successful colleague or superior without trying to find ways to enlist the active participation of their own staff. One way of achieving this is by modeling employees' potential routes to personal fulfillment within the framework of the organization's common goal.

Thus, executives must behave like a salesman, which some may deem a necessary evil. The reason they choose to follow this 'sales' approach is that, at the end of the day, they're responsible for ensuring the work gets done.

The supervisor may be tempted to resort to social and psychological tactics, essentially tricking their employees into performing. This gets the work done, but it doesn't help establish healthy, long-term relationships. In any business, the point isn't to profit on one side but, rather, mutually. If a service is offered for monetary exchange, then both parties participating stand to gain something.

Salesmen thrive on this because their work requires them to identify the needs of the customer. The sales rep must make sure to understand his customers on a basic level and then provide a product that will fulfill their needs. The ability to anticipate the needs of the consumers should make a salesman a superior executive in administrative dealings with people.

Yet, the opposite occurs. Salesmen end up taking pride in outwitting their customers, hence why they usually enjoy hoodwinking their customers by playing on their motives and their interests. When workers come to identify their executives are behaving this way, it is only a matter of time before they start losing interest - moving on to other things.

An executive need to use his skills and human insight to illustrate & capture individual satisfaction in the common enterprise and to create fulfillment that keeps the subordinate engaged. No cute tricks, shortcuts, or halfhearted tactics will accomplish this.

Leadership does not entirely revolve around being in charge or telling others what they should be doing. It involves creating growth opportunities for people without causing anarchy. Leaders are to provide recognition of roles and functions within the group that will permit each member to satisfy and fulfill some major motive or interest.

Dr. Moses Haregewoyn

Chapter Nine - The Millennial Generation

Today's world has certainly come a long way, and the scope of those changes has made things ridiculously advanced. Our ancestors could have never imagined being able to talk to someone from another corner of the world with a touch of a few buttons. However, with accelerated evolution and development, people, ideas, and ways of life have also drastically changed. Sometimes navigating it all can be quite tricky.

This had happened many times before when societies had to evolve based on a new discovery. In the early days, the agricultural revolution was one of the most significant changes.

Now that people could grow their own food, nomadic movement reduced considerably, and villages began forming. Over the years, villages turned into cities, and currently, we essentially have a considerable metropolis spanning the globe.

Then came the industrial revolution, which brought with it many new innovations. Social changes had to adapt to them, and hence we saw the developments of 'working hours and toiling methodically.

The pace of work was accelerated, and yields increased tenfold. Populations began to move towards the cities creating issues of crime, integration among different communities, and the formulation of public education.

Today we have the digital revolution, furthering the way we function in our day-to-day lives. This involves work and the manner of interaction we have with others. Like most developments, there are inherent pros and cons, but the issue is that the upcoming generation finds itself in a period fraught with difficulty.

The world has never been so divided as it is now, and the cultural shift has made matters quite chaotic. The excessive use of technological equipment has affected physical and mental health, along with the common work culture that has so many young people sitting at a desk for hours on end.

It is expected for a person to be passionate and a bit lost during their youth, but the millennials' growth in certain matters has become somewhat stunted. Within the culture, there has been a high rise in divorce rates, suicides, depression, and feelings of alienation. Traits were rare prior to the turn of the century, comparatively speaking.

Many members of the millennial generation find themselves feeling angry, lost, adrift, anxious, and unaware of what they should be doing. This has created a sense of being lost for a protracted period.

Another shift that may contribute to the problems is the shift from religion to science. Since the latter subject has helped contribute to so many unique innovations, many are inexorably drawn to it. This has come at the cost of people nurturing their souls.

Spirituality within the youth has declined. There are cases when a few possess some form of faith, but a considerable sum of this generation has been subject to radicalization not solely only limited to religion but to politics too.

Every day there is an ongoing debate between radical Leftists and conservative Right Wingers. Disagreements between the two ideologies have always existed, but the degree hasn't reached such volatile conditions. People generally turn into enemies over the slightest disputes. People would participate in fiery debates years back, but later on, you would see them having a cup of tea and sharing a few laughs.

Nowadays, even hinting at the possibility of seeing things differently causes a substantial negative reaction. The decline of tolerance pushes people into a chaotic, some may say even catastrophic, situation.

In the middle of so many issues stands the millennial generation that straddles the pre-internet/internet age. They have benefitted from it but suffered as well. They have witnessed more freedom in their workplace but also have suffered with the excessive working hours where physical movement is limited, and duties rely heavily on the internet.

Social interactions are decreasing due to the generation spending more time on their phones. A subsequent dependence on dopamine has led to higher doses of anxiety and depression, causing a cycle of unprecedented problems.

This begs the question that with so many issues looming, how will the young blood manage to persevere through such harsh times as the former generation enters their winter years and retires from the workforce? The excessive levels of intolerance, hypersensitivity, directionless, and constant worrying bring a source of concern on how the world will continue ahead and what kind of precedent the millennial generation will set for the ones to come after.

Cost of Workplace Distractions to Labor Productivity

A workplace has the primary purpose and function of gathering workers to engage in productive efforts that collectively achieve the mission of their employing organization. Employees may be gathered through various channels and different platforms - virtually or physically - yet the dual purpose of the work environment remains contribution and productivity.

Unless the work can be done remotely, many workplaces tend to be at different locations as compared to the place of residence. This is typically done to establish an atmosphere where employees can concentrate on the work being done as opposed to maintaining productivity amid distraction by extraneous developments in their homes unrelated to their jobs.

Any form of distraction negatively impacts employees. This includes the use of cell phones during work time for personal reasons, workers engaging in non-work-related Internet

Leadership: An Incumbent of Faith

browsing during work hours, unproductive socializing with colleagues or gossip during the hours of work, the use of social media for purposes unrelated to their paid work, personal email communication, non-contributory and non-constructive meetings, smoke or snack breaks outside the official breaks, noisy or distractive co-workers.

All forms of distraction that impact the effective or efficient contribution to the needs of the business will, in the long run, have an impact on labor productivity. Labor productivity is the real economic output per labor hour provided and the potential production any given laborer could produce within that hour of work. This, in effect, is the total productivity generated by an employee who is not distracted and has devoted all their attention and resources to their assigned tasks. All things being equal, within working hours, labor productivity will inevitably be affected by the introduction and employee accessibility to their social media accounts and handheld devices.

This is based on the notion that a portion of the time that would have been used for work is diverted to something else. When applied to the workplace, social media distraction refers to the process by which social media prompts and draws the workers' attention away from a task they originally pursued.

When unnecessary diversions occur during work hours, it becomes something in which any cost-reducing business and department should take interest.

As it relates to opportunity costs, if this time dedicated to productivity is given up and invested in personal usage of technological devices, then the ultimate cost is averse to the needs of the business.

This has become a lot more important to today's enterprises as social media distractions and distractions connected to the use of portable handheld devices increase the immediate availability of the Internet, technological advancements, and cheaper technology.

As technological advancements continue to emerge and expand, organizations attempt to update their rules and workplace policies accordingly.

As recent as the 1970s, technology was relatively expensive, mainly because it was in its infancy. However, due to technological innovation and other factors, we now have devices like portable personal computers, laptops, tablets, smartphones, smart washing machines, room sensors, internet-connected cameras, WIFI-enabled cars, and more.

The good news for consumers is that many of the once-expensive devices are getting more affordable for the average worker. Some of the reasons behind the price movements lie in the lack of innovation by developers and manufacturers during the production of these devices.

The lack of innovation means a lot more people are getting to use their devices for a longer time, and new entrants into the markets are able to produce similar alternatives to existing products, which leads producers to reduce product pricing, ensuring an attractive lure to consumers.

Recent technological progress, the interconnectivity of things, and the need to stay in contact with others have led to most workers owning and developing a reliance on electronic devices. The ownership per worker, comparatively, would have increased with time. As well, the affordability of these current devices has contributed to their omnipresence in many workplaces.

Couple with this the fact that many of these devices are much easier to use, relative to the first-generation devices introduced decades ago, and small enough to be carried in a pocket.

There are instances, in some workplaces, where employees' duties are conducted with the use of handheld and portable devices, which makes it difficult to parse the amount of paid time used for work-related responsibilities versus that which is used for personal matters.

This is especially difficult when there are no restrictions to accessing common social media sites and applications. On the one hand, many employees may argue for a need to stay in contact with their families and others, even at work, especially in case of emergencies or parenting situations that inevitably arise. On the other hand, some may claim that such calls could be channeled through official office contacts.

It may, however, be worth considering that some workers may not be comfortable having their personal matters transmitted through office phone lines, especially when they can afford that privacy by simply using their own devices. Further, some offices may not be happy to accommodate the use of their paid resources for personal matters, especially during paid work hours, over and above break, and lunch times.

The increase in the number of handheld devices at the workplace is motivated by various factors. The core motivations for social media and portable handheld device use at work have been to communicate with others, to stay in touch with others, to feel connected, to escape, or to pass the time.

While the use of smart electronic devices does provide positive contributions to the workplace, there are those individuals whose work-related duties do not call for such a prescription or accommodation and may be observed to use personal hand-held devices for passing the time or amusement. This becomes counterproductive to the mission and purposes of the businesses.

Most employers will, therefore, not be supportive of any habit or allocation of resources that can be used for these purposes. They will progressively take steps to ensure that such incidences are limited or eliminated from that place of work because the firm that has employed them will be encountering opportunity costs and loss of paid hours of productive work. This is often referred to as social media distraction.

Workplace social media accessibility or handheld device use and productivity is complex and challenging to analyze.

There is difficulty in calculating the productivity hour losses due to distractions in some places, differing regulations dependent upon regions, the absence of effective policy enforcing agents, the absence of labor hour analytical systems, a relaxed culture that allows the use of personal devices in workplaces, and the belief for many that personal media use actually improves productivity amongst many other reasons.

Some jobs are directly connected to and require the use of social media. These will include jobs where prospective customers contact the organizations through social media. Some job leads are also received through referrals and personal contacts.

Due in part to the accessibility of the Internet, calculating how much paid time is squandered on personal communication via portable devices is difficult. The workplace that does not have access restrictions or limitations may receive both professional and personal emails, text messages, and app notifications during the working day. These outside distractions are of concern for any organization.

The setup and design of social media platforms and apps are such that they engage the users for a prolonged amount of time without the user realizing how much time is being spent. Just like with many things, the increasing use of social media with its addictive dopamine feedback loop has a strong pull and appeal, presenting temptations that encourage distraction.

Social media addiction is associated with negative consequences such as reduced productivity, unhealthy social relationships, and diminishing satisfaction with life. One of the primary effects is that it can lead an individual to override their primary goals and tasks. When an employee becomes distracted, their hazard perception and recognition are influenced. The leading critical factor hypothesized to affect hazard recognition and safety performance is 'distraction.'

Workplace distractions can negatively affect hazard recognition, safety risk perception, and safety performance within construction.

Dr. Moses Haregewoyn

The fact is that some workplaces and environments like construction have workers exposed to numerous emerging technologies such as drones, mobile devices, and intelligent robots.

Any form of distraction could have material implications that can potentially multiply the number of hazards in the work environment. When workers are able to identify, manage or eliminate risks, most construction accidents are preventable.

Given the nature of human beings and the expression of individuality, the reasons for handheld device usage, and by extension, social media, are varied overall. In reducing the minutia of individualism, the bottom line to this issue is a lack of worker self-control, or the person may have a social media use problem that lies at the heart of worker-related distraction and escapist behavior through the usage of these personal devices.

Subsequently, every individual worker may be prone, averse, or neutral to the presence of and availability of portable devices at the workplace. Some may already have their own time management and self-management systems that keep them on track.

Leadership: An Incumbent of Faith

For such a group of people, external control and restrictions may not be as effective, efficient, or necessary.

However, for those who may be prone to using these devices instead of concentrating on their paid work, there may be the need to provide a structured workplace that encourages more focus and work efforts put towards the duties and responsibilities for which they are being paid.

With mobile internet penetration surging, the use of social media in the workplace and neglecting work has also increased. Distractions from work have not all been known to be negative on productivity if used responsibly as it does have some mental health benefits to the workers, which in turn impacts their work.

Some have been considered to have a positive impact on work in appropriate situations: such as socialization, water, breaks, Internet surfing, listening to music, reading, short sleep (power naps), social media, quick phone calls, potluck, lunch, snack, meditation, exercises including stretching and breathing, games, vision board, fun activities, having a clean work area, creating a to-do list.

In some workplaces, these may be done for the workers. Behind these apparent distractions are team-building distractions that ensure the workers have a healthy and positive body and mind or distractions that ensure that workers are getting enough exercise.

The internet is perhaps the most creative innovation ever made in the history of technology. Internet platforms, inclusive of the various social media outlets, have numerous advantages for employers and employees. Much of the work in workplaces is internet-dependent, and the applications and processes available simply enhance the aspects of work.

However, its drawbacks in certain areas, particularly employee productivity, surface areas of concern as to whether the internet through surveillance processes impacts workers' productivity or not.

Many organizations turn to surveillance in the workplace in pursuit of improved workplace productivity through monitoring the activities of their employees. Monitoring employees is one strategy to keep track of their productivity during work hours and the utilization of their time in doing what they were paid to do.

Employers would often want to know what their employees are doing during working hours to make sure their time is not taken up by distractions.

Leadership: An Incumbent of Faith

The implication of workplace surveillance is initially advantageous to tracking productivity. Employees are less likely to be unproductive when they know they are being monitored as they will be inclined to emphasize making an impression to their employer that they, in fact, are being productive employees upon observance.

Controversies with workplace surveillance generally arise when observation goes beyond what is reasonable and necessary.

Consequently, surveillance at the workplace impacts employee productivity in a positive way as it cultivates a productive work culture.

Productivity can drastically increase when employees are aware of their work being monitored through surveillance systems. Employees are more inclined to impress their employer when they know their work is being observed.

Employees are more likely to work towards providing a productive day at work when there is an incentive in place for productivity.

Defining Generations

Let's begin with getting an understanding of generational differences. A generation is a group that can be identified by the year of birth, age, location, and significant life events such as wars, new technologies, or major economic transitions. These events form the personality, values, and expectations of that generation.

Over the past seven decades, there have been three generations dominating the workplace. Baby Boomers, Generation X, and Generation Y (Millennials).

The ones growing up somewhat behind Millennials are called Generation Z, or Gen-Z.

The Baby Boomer generation is anyone born between 1943 and 1960. They are given this name because when men returned from WW2, there was an increase in birth rates, hence creating a baby boom. Baby Boomers were raised in a prosperous economic time.

This generation, unlike the current one, did not grow up dependent on technology.

Leadership: An Incumbent of Faith

Generation X was born between 1961 and 1979. It marks the period of birth decline after the baby boom and is significantly smaller than in previous and succeeding generations. Generation X was the first latchkey generation, i.e., children who returned home from school without a parent to greet them.

Two working parents had become the norm. Culturally speaking, this generation grew up in an environment of rising crime, increasing divorce rates, and economic instability.

Millennials, individuals born between 1980 and 2000, are currently entering the workforce and are labeled as such due to being born at the turn of the century. Strongly influenced by technology, they've been formed in (and by) a global, digitally connected era.

Generally speaking, this diverse influx of data from the world wide web may be partially responsible for their greater acceptance of non-traditional identities, families, and cultural values.

Dr. Moses Haregewoyn

The Importance of Understanding Millennials

In the upcoming years, the Baby Boomer generation will be replaced by Millennials, who are expected to dominate the workplace. Misunderstandings between generations can detrimentally affect employee performance and satisfaction.

Managers must learn about their employees' job satisfaction and organizational commitment levels as a new generation merge with the older established ones.

In order to attract and retain Millennials, it's essential for a manager or organization to understand what motivates and satisfies the younger generation.

Differences between generations can create problems such as distrust among employees and high turnover rates. These problems make it vital to understand Millennials' values and demands. Understanding generational differences are helpful in negotiating workplace conflicts, if not avoiding them entirely.

The potential for interpersonal friction resulting from differences in values and expectations is high. If these are not addressed or identified, more discord is sure to follow.

Values & Characteristics of Millennials

There are many positive and negative qualities shared by the Millennial generation. More than anything, Millennials are confident. This confidence stems from their trust and optimism.

However, over time as the harsher realities of 'adulting' set in, they become more nihilistic and easily aggravated, leading to disillusion which manifests in an increased turnover rate.

Millennials are known to be achievement focused. They have a need not only to do well but to excel and surpass all goals and aspirations. This inspires them to pursue new learning opportunities. Some believe that this novelty-seeking behavior leads to rudderless conduct up to and including a willingness to resign based on principal.

Yet, many millennials are willing to put forth the extra effort to help an organization succeed. Not only are they generally achievement-focused, but they feel accountable for their actions, too. The education system has helped contribute a sense of accountability, but in recent years, blame has been distributed and externally assigned instead of taking ownership of missteps.

Dr. Moses Haregewoyn

Some notable traits amongst millennials are the desire to work in teams exhibiting a dearth of tolerance for individual differences that exceed that of prior generations. This is because most of its members have been raised in sports teams, standardized testing, and group learning, so it's not surprising that this trait follows them in the workplace. This aspect of teamwork has made its members more tolerant of certain things that perhaps the former generation did not approve of, such as tattoos on women. This tolerance has been implemented due to growing up in more diverse environments and working in teams that give new perspectives. Yet this tolerance adheres to specific things because there is a lot of disagreement and conflict between one another.

Millennials enjoy utilizing technology. The Millennial generation became dependent on technology at an earlier age than other generations. Similar to learning a new language, people who utilize technology at an earlier age become more proficient than people who understand it later in their life. It is assumed that as more Millennials begin taking over the workplace, the more integrated technology will be in work processes.

Leadership: An Incumbent of Faith

There are plenty of complaints targeted at Millennials from Baby Boomers who can be difficult to interact with, are entitled, and overly service-focused. This comes from the new generation expressing opinions and making greater demands than their elder, more 'experienced' counterparts.

Millennials are also referenced as the 'look at me generation' because they are considered too overconfident and concerned with their own interests. In opinion polls, the younger generations are perceived to be impatient, lacking in work ethic, self-important and disloyal.

Millennials may attempt to gain influential positions in large projects soon after being hired. Coworkers can be taken aback by this, believing it to be arrogance driving the new generation and not simply their need to 'overachieve.'

Millennials' expectancy of work/life balance has, at times, created conflict with Baby Boomer coworkers; this conflict could be the background mentality that Millennials are 'selfish and lazy.' The need for work/life balance makes older generations doubt Millennials concerning organizational commitment and dedication. Analysts also found that as Millennials place more focus on their outside lives, Baby Boomers may begin to question the sacrifices they've made for their careers.

Older employees may begin taking a greater interest in their own private lives, or additional conflicts may arise from these differing personal values.

Millennials in the Workplace

Due to the recent recession of 2008 and the longer average lifespan of the standard American, people are working longer than compared to any other time in the nation's history. As a result, organizations must understand how newer generations compare and work with previous generations. An example of this is the valuation different generations place on leadership qualities in the workplace.

While ambition is found to be the most esteemed quality for Baby Boomers and Gen X, the Millennial generation favors a thoughtful, considerate boss above any other qualities. They also prefer their managers to be inspiring and imaginative. Overall, Millennials want a more interpersonal relationship with their management and to know that their manager cares.

Leadership: An Incumbent of Faith

Also, Millennials desire a flexible work environment with fewer rules and regulations. With a high confidence level, Millennials feel they need less regulation to guide their decisions.

For the Millennial generation, confidence is expressed not only in how they perform but in how they view themselves. Compared to older generations, Millennials are less likely to identify themselves as overweight even though they have a much higher rate of obesity and less overall fitness.

This can significantly affect the workplace as the newer generation begins to take control. If not dealt with, there can be an increase in health and care costs, not to mention illness-related absences.

The economic crash in 2008 affected both Millennials and Baby Boomers differently. The decline in housing prices and drops in the stock market have reduced retirement portfolios. Due to this, the Baby Boomer generation is finding it difficult to retire and must stay in their positions for longer than they had hoped. Generation X now cannot promote because the Baby Boomer isn't leaving, and the economy is stunted.

Dr. Moses Haregewoyn

Without the economy's growth, older generations stay put in their positions, while the Millennials find themselves in a strange, awkward limbo state without the ability to gain valuable experience.

If a manager prefers to employ a Millennial who will stay for a longer period of time, then a graduate degree is the preferred standard. Millennials who have a graduate degree are more likely to stay longer, carry better self-confidence and achieve higher job satisfaction.

Due to the recessions, Millennials have been experiencing a diminishing sense of job security. Millennials understand that job security and retirement after working for one organization are rare.

This mentality has led Millennials to seek out new employment opportunities more frequently, and so Millennials take a more proactive approach towards making themselves more enticing to the job market. By simply offering some mention of short-term or longer-term security, a manager may increase employee commitment level.

Millennials tend to have higher expectations for advancement opportunities within their careers. Due to the generations' confidence and the subsequent need to overachieve, they are more likely to seek career-enhancing opportunities in an organization.

By offering advancement opportunities, organizations may also retain their talent. Since enhancement opportunities are important to this newer generation, training and development sessions can be valuable retention and motivational tools. Mentoring and training are also highly valued and appreciated by the Millennials. This satisfies their need to develop new skills and marketability but also creates greater job satisfaction and productivity.

Millennials may have difficulty earning respect and credibility from the older generations in the workplace. Many negative stereotypes follow this generation, and a lack of understanding of these differences can hurt them even more. Millennials are wise in apprehending their coworkers' opinions and making an effort to demonstrate their actual value.

One thing that truly sets the newer generation apart is their preference for meaningful work over well-paid work. At the same time, salary is still important in determining success; work that has meaning and enjoyment in what one does is rated higher in importance than financial gain. Furthermore, millennials rank social awareness high vis a vis organizational obligation and prefer work that is socially responsible.

Perhaps this is also a cause of the recession, be that as it may, Millennials tend toward meaningful and challenging jobs that can potentially advance their career.

Generational Differences

Despite the many new and unique qualities of the young blood, there is still little difference between generations in the workforce today. Many of the differences presented exist due to prejudice that, in recent years, has seeped into the culture as a reaction to fear of change.

Generations are found to be more alike than different, and the differences between them are over-exaggerated. Every generation has been chastised by the generation before them. Baby Boomers have a tendency to complain about Millennials using slang, social rights, and tolerance, just as the WW2 generation criticized Baby Boomers over the same topics. The beliefs of older generations about younger generations have persisted for the past forty years.

182

Leadership: An Incumbent of Faith

Work/life balance is an example of an over-exaggerated difference between generations. The greater need for work/life balance derives from the person's stage of life and not from the generation in which they were born. So instead of a person wanting more time at home because they were born in 1988, it may be because they need to take care of their baby.

A Baby Boomer may need a better work/life balance because they must take care of an elder parent in a nursing home. This shows that the need for a great work/life balance can hold true for anyone, not just isolated generational needs.

Most research written on Millennials integrating into the workplace comes from trade magazines and practitioner articles. Practitioners are like scholarly authors who believe in the importance of understanding generational differences. With the growing number of Millennials entering an aging workforce and the conflict that can arise from generational differences, many practitioners are writing editorials vis a vis Millennials and what organizations expect.

Practitioners agree that Millennials are technologically advanced and tend to incorporate technology into the fabric of their personal and professional lives. An employer may become frustrated after seeing an employee texting at a meeting or surfing the web with their smartphone.

For Millennials, using technology and social media is natural and essential. However, Millennials may be using their technical knowledge and ability to use social media to find answers to the question they have. Due to this, Millennials not only require strong use of technology at work but must also have it in portable form. Unfortunately, the use of technology has also negatively impacted the Millennial generation because they now expect to have everything instantly.

With internet speed providing instant access to any answer, this generation now expects to have immediate responses and real-time feedback.

Practitioners tend to have issues when it comes to matters regarding feedback. Millennials have a dependency on a continuous feedback loop. When it isn't readily offered, they'll automatically assume that their work isn't up to the mark. The continuous need for feedback can lead to surprise and frustration in an organization.

The Millennials' dependence on feedback stems from 'helicopter parenting, where parents are in a routine of monitoring and coddling their child to a certain degree. They have a tendency to continuously push their children, give constant feedback, and tend to be shielding. Attempting to bolster the child's self-esteem, sometimes to the detriment, parents strive to instill a sense of 'specialness' within their youngsters. The term 'trophy kid' derives from the idea (turned into policy in some areas) that children deserve trophies for simply participating in any given activity.

Practitioners believe that Millennials, due to their upbringing, require a more structured organization where they are told what to do and when to do it. They even expect organizations to take an interest in their ideas so that the organization will develop a reliance on them.

Practitioners agree that Millennials desire a good work/life balance. They have found that Millennials will trade a higher profile and a higher paying job for one that is more elastic and allows for time at home when it is needed. A Millennial requires a more open position and will generally choose their personal life over professional responsibilities.

When this newer generation begins to take hold of the workplace, the traditional nine-to-five day will become more elastic and suited to the individual's needs. Millennials gravitated to this value and need for work/life balance by seeing their parents sacrifice their home lives only to fall victim to downsizing.

Practitioners also agree on two other values Millennials desire from an organization. First, Millennials desire to work for a company that is socially responsible.

Working for a company that helps people has become a top priority for Millennials. They genuinely desire to help others and prefer a mission-driven organization that feels the same. Additionally, teamwork is valued among Millennials.

Through team learning in schools, Millennials have developed the ability and value the opportunity to work in such a fashion. This generation's value system of teamwork has also instilled a greater tolerance of other people's races, nationalities, and gender preferences.

While the practitioners have their fair share of merit in their research, they still fail to back their opinions up with solid empirical evidence. What this information does provide is an understanding of the viewpoints of a workforce. It also provides the reason why more research needs to be conducted to understand the true differential behaviors in generations coexisting in the workforce.

Implications

Due to the growing natural influx of the upcoming generation, it will become crucial for managers to adapt their leadership style to the motivational needs of Millennials.

The values identified can be used to develop recommended practice guidelines. Companies will benefit from the Millennials' achievement-focused mentality, as this generation puts forth extra effort to help an organization succeed. Managers will also need to provide career-enhancing opportunities; otherwise, other companies may scalp quality employees. Managers may have to provide ongoing, real-time feedback, or Millennials will assume their work is substandard.

Millennials desire work that has meaning. Enjoyment in what one does rates higher in importance than financial gains for this generation. If a company continues to assign meaningless tasks, it may find itself with a high turnover. Companies also need to provide teamwork opportunities.

The Millennials' utilization of teamwork will provide the opportunity to gain new perspectives in getting a project completed. Companies can also expect to see an increase in the utilization of technology. Millennials became dependent on technology at an early age, so technology integration will become even more prominent as Millennials take over.

Empathy is a trait that is needed heavily by the young generation. Millennials desire a caring employer who wishes to build more interpersonal relationships. To avoid high turnover, companies will have to be less ambitious and more connected to their employees' needs. The caveat here is that Millennials value focusing on family and their private lives instead of their careers, which may create issues for companies.

If a company does not accept this shift in values, then that company may find Millennial retention difficult. As companies are seeing, Millennials require a flexible work environment with fewer rules and regulations.

Due to these differences in values, among other generational variations, companies can expect to see complaints and conflict arise as Millennials' employment numbers increase. One common complaint is that Millennials resent/avoid difficulties and are entitled.

This perception results from Millennials' propensity to express opinions and make greater demands than their older, more experienced counterparts.

Leadership: An Incumbent of Faith

Millennials may come across as lacking in work ethic because they gain important positions soon after being hired. Other generations may believe that Millennials are selfish and lazy because Millennials place a higher priority on their lives outside the workplace.

Due to the negative stereotyping and misunderstandings of their values, Millennials will find it challenging to earn respect. Companies will need to make an effort to appreciate the differences in values. To properly avoid conflict and maintain motivation, the desire to understand each of your coworkers will prove essential.

Chapter Ten - The Future of Leadership

The future is always uncertain. Nobody can predict it. At best, the one thing we can do is expect the unexpected, but sometimes, certain roles in society cannot be left to the whims of fate. Leadership is one of those things.

We have seen how effective leadership technique has slowly evolved over the years, and now people prefer a more team-work-oriented environment where the leader has a genuine relationship with those around him. Gradually, over time, the archetypes of the lone office manager and traditional bureaucratic hierarchy have waned. Many, in fact, believe that managers might no longer exist in the workplace after some years.

This begs the question, if certain traits of the working environment are expected to change, how will that affect leadership in general? Will the dynamic now shift from one person to a completely democratic style of leading others?

Will someone still have certain authority over others, or will that conception be eliminated? Would assigning tasks instead be left in the hands of technology rather than a person?

These are things we need to be willing to consider as we face a glut of change that seems to precipitate and accelerate with each passing year. People need to know how to adapt lest they be overwhelmed, and forward momentum is frustrated.

In current times, it seems we've reached the end of management as we know it because the technology of management has now reached a peak.

As active leaders of the workforce, we must work out how to coordinate the efforts of thousands of individuals without creating a burdensome hierarchy of overseers. Modern management, especially leadership, is not limited to a static set of tools and techniques; it's a dynamic paradigm. This leadership paradigm entails a view that the essential function of leaders is to direct and control. This control is exercised by eliminating uncertainty and by dealing with negative deviations from the grand plan.

Leaders then need to understand the entire system, see its connections, foresee the responses of people and, from this, design and execute appropriate interventions.

Dr. Moses Haregewoyn

The mainstream methods and tools of modern leadership and management were invented to solve the problems of control and efficiency. We'll envision leadership in the future as serving the objective of multiplying human accomplishment in a world of growing uncertainty, accelerating change, and mounting complexity.

We are closing in on becoming a 'post-managerial' society, maybe even a 'post-organizational' one. This begs the question, what is the future of leadership itself?

Post-Managerial Society with Rising Complexity

The current paradigms predominately reflect the assumption that leadership involves processes of intentional influence exerted by an appointed person over others to facilitate the activities of workers within an organization.

A leader, sitting outside their organization as an objective individual, can design and apply deliberate interventions to move the organization or group of people forward.

Today, it's nearly impossible to identify the preferred attributes of a modern 'ideal leader.'

Leadership: An Incumbent of Faith

Given this, it would be erroneous to conclude that a person with the requisite desirable attributes would perform effectively as a leader.

How the leader performs depends just as much on the character of the recognition they receive and the nature of those responses elicited from others (feedback) as it does on these 'personal attributes.'

When it comes to traditional leadership, large amounts of focus have been placed on control as well as manipulations of social systems.

Considering how omnipresent technology has become in our daily lives, it cannot be denied that the complexities have too.

They've skyrocketed in many ways.

This can be seen in organizations currently in the following manner:

- Whether private or public, organizations operate in a complex external and internal environment. Vital assumptions continuously change due to dynamic developments and events.

Dr. Moses Haregewoyn

- Organizations will become enriched in employee diversity, structure, activities, processes, and culture.

- Organizations behave like perpetually evolving organisms- there is often no single 'shape' or 'reality' leaders can unanimously decide on.

- People build a future that reflects their history, identity, and agenda but which is always open to further shaping as people continue to communicate and interact.

- People shape their future not as a single 'vision,' values, or strategy but in terms of what actions become possible and sensible for them, given their circumstances.

- People in the organization influence and affect each other through loops of interaction that create individual and collective motivation, behavior, and identity. These influences arise in dynamic relationships between people and in specific and changing contexts.

- People are continually shaping and shifting the width and depth of their relationships, depending on the context; individuals and groups form and are formed by each other simultaneously.

- Some members of their respective organizations are not the rational actors their leaders wish them to be. They behave and react in a number of unpredictable ways.

As time passes, leaders will not always have the choices and control that the prevailing leadership paradigm has allowed. In a world of growing complexity, the best a leader can do is channel their intentions into interactions with their followers, and through group efforts, a new mode/paradigm/protocol/goal is created. This may be so because the future is also evolving, and the past is incessantly reconstructed in relation to the present moment.

Therefore, we cannot fully determine what happens or choose it, regardless of any clever foresight methods or tools. This does not necessarily mean that there is no personal freedom or choice.

We as leaders can have intentions and be purposeful about our intentions in relation to others. There is still plenty of room for leadership to be around in the years to come, but it most certainly will take a different form.

Dr. Moses Haregewoyn

Identity Formation

In recent years, the positioning, structural, and power configuration of leadership decreased in importance, and the future concept of leadership will contain other elements. One of these is identity formation. The kind of leaders that we follow tend to be reflections of our own identities.

The way we talk in a group or in an organization reflects how we see ourselves in the workplace. New methods of talking are new ways of making sense of the people around us.

People communicate with one another to couple their practical activities in the workplace with those around them to create meaning and express identity. In these attempts, people are constructing relationships.

People develop and sustain specific ways of relating to each other in their conversations and then, from conversations, make sense of their surroundings and themselves. When leaders influence the way people talk in organizations, they construct new forms of relationships, and to construct new forms of relationships is to create new ways of being ourselves.

Leadership: An Incumbent of Faith

During this phase of people interacting with one another, a leader is generally formed. The leader is as much formed by the group as he or she forms the group in his or her recognition of others. The role of the leader emerges and is continually iterated in social processes of recognition. The act of leadership will more and more be created simultaneously between leaders and followers as complexity increases.

In the future, the concept of leadership will be better understood as a dynamic process that occurs between people rather than depending on the individual characteristics of the leadership role. Today's general obsession with the characteristics of the leadership role is coupled with a tendency to see an organization in terms of its leader, to locate the responsibility for the life of an organization, in its broadest sense, with an extraordinary individual.

Leadership is not static or permanently conferred but, rather, emerges from the ongoing interaction between leaders and followers in the present. What we need to recognize is that the leader-follower relationship is a configuration of power in which the power balance is tilted toward the leader. This one who is recognized as a leader is one who has the capacity to influence the group.

197

This kind of ability can never be static. The potential for a shift in power is, therefore, present in any given moment as long as there's interaction going on. Whoever is momentarily taking the lead will be dependent upon the individual(s) presently able to make a tentative sense of what is happening. The reason for this paradoxical nature in modern leadership arises from the complex process of being and not being in control. Acknowledging feelings of not being in control is essential to a process that enables others to act.

Leaders' struggle to hold on to a sense of order in a chaotic world is linked to a desire to reduce anxieties associated with disorder and unpredictability. In their anxieties, leaders, and employees alike want to believe that someone, somewhere, is in control.

However, the notion of the leader as the one who is in control is not consistent with reality. Precious leadership time and effort will, in the future, be better spent on paying attention to identity and relationship issues.

The concept of leadership will, in the future, be about dealing with the unknown and the emergence of new patterns of communication and behavior. Hence, the action of the leader is not split from the nature of leadership, and we contend that the future of leadership will be best understood as a shift from 'idealized' to the 'actual' experience between people.

Leaders emerge in the interaction between people as the act of recognizing and being recognized, as well as the act of gaining the necessary trust, credibility, and respect to perform as a leader. Leadership is then an emergent phenomenon of people in interaction. The leader is embodied in an individual person, but leadership is a social phenomenon that emerges only in interaction and has no value without interaction.

Paying Attention to Relationships

The future concept of leadership will emerge not only as a function of identity but also as a result of relationships. This is the forming and being formed relationship between leaders and followers in a group.

Recent developments in the field of neuroscience have shown that we live in constant relationships with other people and that these people play a part in regulating our social and emotional behavior. The human brain itself is a social organ, and brains themselves exist and develop in relationship to other brains.

Such shifting relationships between people in a group are predominately governed by dynamic, social, cognitive, and coordination/power-related psychological processes.

A leader must keep in mind that the psychological processes in question are not manageable but emerge between people influenced by communication as a result of a complex mixture of motivation, trust, feelings, emotions, group norms, knowledge acquisition, learning, sense-making, as well as a complex and soft power play.

Taking account of relationships in the act of leading is better understood as leading by acting in the moment but at the same time paying attention to our experience. This involves allowing for thinking and feeling self in the presence of others. This occurs through listening to one's own physical, cognitive, and emotional responses and factoring these into the leadership process. This is called 'leading reflexively.'

When a leader employs this, they influence processes on an identity level where personal stakes may be high. It certainly wouldn't be unfair to state that future leadership isn't for everyone.

Leadership: An Incumbent of Faith

This is so because successful leaders frame their life stories in ways that allow them to see themselves not as passive observers in life but as individuals who determinedly develop self–awareness from their personal histories.

Not everyone has the capacity to transform their experiences into something of value to form a unique and effective way of leading.

Not everyone will necessarily connect with a leader's way of framing his or her experiences into anecdotal evidence for outstanding leadership.

The current paradigms of leadership predominately reflect the assumption that it involves a process whereby intentional influence is exerted by an appointed person over other people to facilitate activities in a group of people or in an organization.

For a very long time, we became pretty accustomed to the standard assembly-line style learning method, which was a result of the industrial revolution. Now with the digital revolution taking place, the question 'what's next' arises.

Dr. Moses Haregewoyn

As mentioned before, in our current times, the environment has changed too much, too fast. The skills required of a leader are far more complex and require quicker adaptation than ever.

Despite our reliance on digital technology, the methods currently employed to develop leaders haven't changed much.

Most managers are forged from on-the-job experiences, training, and coaching/mentoring. These do offer their benefits, but at the current rate, they aren't developing leaders fast enough.

This creates challenges for what awaits us. It isn't only a leadership issue but one of development.

Managers have become experts on the 'what' of leadership but still don't have a tight grip on the 'how' of their own development.

If the future is to be taken head-on, then there are four trends that are important for leadership development which are:

- Focusing on vertical development.

- Transference of greater developmental ownership to the individual.

- More focus on the collective rather than individual leadership.

- More work on innovation in leadership development methods.

Focusing on Vertical Developmental

There are two different types of development-horizontal verticals. A great deal of time has been spent on 'horizontal' development but very little time on 'vertical' development.

By shifting focus from competencies towards developmental stages, there is a better fighting chance for leading others in the years to come.

Transference of Greater Developmental Ownership to the Individual

People develop fastest when they feel responsible for their own progress.

The current model encourages people to believe that someone else is responsible for their development, e.g., human resources, their manager, or trainers. We will need to help people out of the passenger seat and into the driver's seat of their own development.

Collective Over Individual Leadership

Leadership development has come to the point of being too focused on an individual. It's become too elitist. There is a transition occurring from the old paradigm in which leadership resides in a person or role to a new one in which leadership is a collective process spread throughout networks of people. The question will change from, 'Who are the leaders?' to 'what conditions do we need for leadership to flourish in the network?'

Innovation in Leadership Development Methods

There are no simple, existing models or programs that will be sufficient to develop the levels of collective leadership to meet an increasingly complex future.

Instead, an era of rapid innovation will be needed in which organizations experiment with new approaches that combine diverse ideas in new ways and share these with others.

Technology and the web will both provide the infrastructure and drive the change. Organizations that embrace the changes will do better than those resisting them.

The current paradigms of leadership predominately reflect the assumption that it involves a process whereby intentional influence is exerted by an appointed person over other people to facilitate activities in a group of people or in an organization.

The Current Crisis

The pace of change and complexity are two main issues regarding leadership in the years to come. The last decade has seen many industries enter a period of increasingly rapid change. This has given rise to the term 'V.U.C.A.'

It's an acronym with origins in the army, and it encapsulates the following traits:

Volatile: Change happens rapidly and on a large scale.

Dr. Moses Haregewoyn

Uncertain: The future cannot be predicted with any precision.

Complex: Challenges are complicated by many factors, and there are few single causes or solutions.

Ambiguous: There is little clarity on what events mean and what effect they may have.

There are several factors that make complex environments challenging to manage:

- A large number of interacting elements.

- Information in the system is highly ambiguous, incomplete, or indecipherable. Interactions among system elements are nonlinear and tightly coupled such that small changes can produce disproportionately large effects.

- Solutions emerge from the dynamics within the system and cannot be imposed from outside with predictable results.

- Hindsight does not lead to foresight since the elements and conditions of the system can be in continual flux.

Some of the most common challenges for future leaders include:

- Information overload.

- The interconnectedness of systems and business communities.

- The dissolving of traditional organizational boundaries.

- New technologies disrupt old work practices.

- The difference in values and expectations of new generations entering the workplace.

- Expanding globalization occasions the need to lead across cultures.

The Required Skillset

In order to function with the complexities around, there are some skills that are vital for leaders to get by, which include:

- Adaptability.

- Self-Awareness.

- Boundary Spanning.

- Collaboration.

- Network Thinking.

In the growing VUCA environment, the demand is starting to shift away from isolated behavioral competencies toward complex 'thinking' abilities. These manifest as adaptive competencies such as learning agility, self-awareness, comfort with ambiguity, and strategic thinking. With such changes in the mental demands on future leaders, the question will become an issue of how we'll produce these capacities of thinking.

The Outdating Methods for Developing Leaders

Currently, organizations are increasingly reliant on HR departments to build a leadership pipeline of managers capable of leading 'creatively' through turbulent times.

However, there appears to be a growing belief among managers and senior executives that the leadership programs being given are not sufficient enough to keep up.

The most common current development methods are:

- Training.

- Job Assignments.

- Action Learning.

- Executive Coaching.

- Mentoring.

- 360-Degree Feedback.

The Development Challenge

Most methods, such as content-heavy training, that are being used to develop leaders for the 21st century have already become dated and redundant. While these were relatively effective for the needs and challenges of the last century, they are becoming increasingly mismatched against the challenges leaders currently face.

There is a distinction between knowing what 'good' leadership is and being able to do it. With the way things are currently going, we face diminishing returns from teaching managers more about leadership when they still have little understanding of what is required for real development to occur.

Increasing Focus on Vertical Development

For quite some time, it's been commonly assumed that leadership development involves establishing and focusing on the competencies, ideally, said leader might have and individually assist those individuals in developing them. In the act of doing so, we have failed to differentiate between the two types of development, vertical and horizontal.

Horizontal development is the development of new skills, abilities, and behaviors. It is technical learning. Horizontal development is most useful when a problem is clearly defined and there are known techniques for solving it. An example of this is surgery training. In this form of training, students become surgeons through a process called 'pimping.'

In this approach, an experienced surgeon fires questions at students until one of them is stumped or gives an incorrect answer. The student is sent back to their books and review/relearn the material while still absorbing any new information that may be presented. The process is by no means easy, but clear answers are easily codified and transmitted from expert sources, allowing the students to broaden and deepen their surgical competency.

Vertical development, on the other hand, refers to the 'stages' that people progress through in regard to how they 'make sense of their world. It is like observing children as we witness them growing older. Although, as humans, we physically tend to stop growing in our twenties, our mental growth continues even after.

There are a series of predictable stages of cognitive development. As the levels get higher, adults get better at making sense of the world around them and its complexities. This is a display of their mind expansion.

Having understood the differences between the two types, a question emerges, 'why should someone's level of cognitive development matter for leadership and organization?'

The answer is that, from a leadership perspective, people at higher levels of development perform better in more complex environments. The reason that managers at higher levels of cognitive development can function more effectively is that they can 'think' in more complex ways.

With each step or rising level, a person can take more challenging scenarios and even bring original solutions.

It paves the way in a new direction and reacting comes easily in times of need.

Causes of Vertical Development

Both horizontal and vertical development differ from one another when it comes to their causes and structure.

Horizontal can be learned from an expert, but vertical development needs to be earned, especially by the person themselves.

It cannot be handed to them. Vertical development is caused by the following:

- People feel consistently frustrated by situations, dilemmas, or challenges in life.

- A sense of having limitations in their current way of thinking.

- A person feels they're in an area that they care deeply about.

- When a source of support exists, enabling them to persist in a time of anxiety and conflict.

Development movement from one stage to the next is usually driven by limitations in the current stage.

When a person is confronted with increased complexity and challenges that can't be reconciled with what you know and can do at her current level, you are pulled to take the next step.

Development accelerates when people can identify the assumptions holding them at their current level of development and test their validity.

This usually all occurs through a three-stage process:

- *Awakening:* The person becomes aware that there is a different way of making sense of the world and that doing things in a new way is possible.

- *Unlearning and discerning:* The old assumptions are analyzed and challenged. New assumptions are tested and subject to experimentation, potentially producing innovative possibilities for one's day-to-day work and life.

- *Advancement:* Occurs after some practice and effort, when new ideas get stronger and start to dominate the previous ones. The new level of development starts to make more sense than the old one.

Leadership Development for Masses

The fact is, every organization needs a leader at some level or another. The flaw remains that most of these people who are set up in such positions only follow what their higher-ups want while tending to nurture an 'elitist' approach.

Leadership development can be democratized if workers get a better understanding of what development is, why it matters to them, and how they can take ownership of their own development.

If organizations believe that their people would not be motivated to take more ownership of their own development, they might stop and ask, 'how clear and visible is the risk/reward for learning in our organization?'

When people start taking more ownership of their own development:

Leadership: An Incumbent of Faith

- They receive recognition from senior leaders that in complex environments, business strategies cannot be executed without highly developed leaders.

- There's buy-in from the senior leaders that new methods for development need to be used and that they will go first and lead by example.

- Staff is willing to be educated on the research of how development occurs and what the benefits are for them

- All staff understands why development works better when they own it.

- There's a realignment of reward systems to emphasize development and performance.

- The utilization of new technologies will allow for control of feedback and provide the ability to collate ongoing suggestions for improvement.

- A culture will be created in which it's safe to take the types of risks required to stretch your mind into the discomfort/learning zone.

Dr. Moses Haregewoyn

The Decline of the Heroic Leader-Rise of Collective Leadership

We all grew up listening to stories of the one hero who led his people to victory. The one-man show was undoubtedly the norm many years back, but with time, this ideal has waned tremendously.

The thought of having a singular, heroic leader leading today doesn't quite work on a daily basis. In times of crisis, it may be necessary. Otherwise, it's simply inviting an authoritarian to call the shots.

Nowadays, many things have become more democratic, and teamwork is preferred. This has both its pros and cons, but for the years to come, it is a given that the collective will be the vanguard, especially in the workplace.

For the past five decades of leadership development, there have been discoveries about 'what' made a good leader, which was followed by a series of practices that helped a generation of individuals move closer to that ideal.

The workplace rewards individuals who can think through a situation analytically and then direct others to carry out strategically planned procedures.

Leadership: An Incumbent of Faith

Leadership has never been easy, but the process itself was comparatively clearer. In recent years, this model's become less effective- archaic.

This is so because the challenges presented by the current socioeconomic environment and the ability of 'heroic' individuals to intervene is in a state of disconnect.

The complexity of the new environment increasingly presents 'adaptive challenges.' In these, it is not possible for any one individual to know the solution or even define the problem.

Instead, adaptive challenges call for collaborative efforts between various stakeholders, each of these maintaining unique worldviews and cosmologies. Many of these stakeholders will- with varying comfortability levels- have to adapt, grow, and unify if they hope to resolve any issue facing their team/workplace.

These collectives, which often cross geographies, reporting lines, and organizations, need to collaboratively share information, create plans, influence each other, and make decisions.

In the current climate, we need to teach those in charge a new range of competencies that focus more on collaboration and influence skills.

Innovation is a result of large numbers of connection points in a network that causes existing ideas to be combined in new ways.

This requirement now is to embrace networks of leadership rather than just one person. The field of innovation has already begun this process.

Redefining Leadership

Leadership can be enacted by anyone; it is not tied to a position of authority in the hierarchy.

Leadership can become free to be distributed throughout networks of people, and across boundaries and geographies, the leader becomes less important than what is needed in the system and how we can produce it.

If leadership is seen as a shared process rather than an individual skill set, senior members must consider the best way to help leadership flourish in their organizations.

Leadership: An Incumbent of Faith

Leadership spread throughout a network of people is more likely to flourish when certain conditions support it. These conditions include:

- Open flows of information.

- Flexible hierarchies.

- Distributed resources.

- Distributed decision-making.

- Loosening of centralized controls.

When organizations choose to embrace these conditions, they will align themselves with the wave of new technologies that are changing the way we work and organize our workplaces. We are still currently in the early stages of thinking about leadership development at a collective level, and it seems increasingly likely that future generations will see leadership residing within networks as a natural phenomenon.

The meteoric rise of the internet and the omnipresence of social networking have helped flatten hierarchies and decentralize control. Nodes of leadership will inevitably manifest throughout the system, so development methods are sure to follow soon after.

How Leadership Looks Different in a Network

In order for organizations to become more effective at using networks of leadership, interviewees suggested a number of changes that would need to occur. First, at the collective level, the goal for an organization would be to create intelligent leadership networks, which can help coalesce and disband in response to various organizational challenges.

These networks might contain people from different geographies, functions, and specializations, both within and external to the organization. Our brains become smarter as the number of neural networks and connections are increased, and organizations that connect more parts of their social system to each other and build a culture of shared leadership will have greater adaptability and collective capacity. Organizations would use their leadership development programs to help people understand that leadership is not contained in isolated job roles but in a process that takes place across a network of people to successively define direction, establish alignment, and garner the commitment of stakeholders.

Leadership: An Incumbent of Faith

While leadership may sometimes be focused on one individual, increasingly, it will be a process that occurs at the team level, with various people's contributions influencing the commitment of the collective. As change happens, the distinction between the leaders and the followers becomes less apparent or relevant. *Everyone* will be *both* at different times.

Organizations could choose to invest their leadership development efforts to improve capacity at one of five different levels:

- Individual capacity.

- Team capacity.

- Organizational capacity.

- Network capacity.

- Systems capacity.

Not all types of organizations will need to adopt this new paradigm of thinking. Traditional companies, in stable environments requiring little creativity from staff, may well be more effective if they stick to traditional, individualistic command and control management styles.

221

However, organizations that expect to operate in VUCA environments will quickly need to develop the types of networks and cultures in which leadership flows through the system. Complex environments will reward flexible and responsive collective leadership.

The time is fast approaching for organizations to redress the imbalance that has been created by focusing exclusively on the individual leadership model.

New Era of Innovation in Leadership Development

In the current era, there are not many models or programs that are capable of producing the levels of leadership capacity needed. This tends to make it easy for organizations to revert to the leadership practices that they've traditionally used.

The creation of new development methods will be an arduous process. Transformations are most likely, to begin with small pockets of innovators within organizations who sense that change is either needed or inevitable.

The innovators will have to be prepared to experiment and fail in order to gain more feedback from which to build their subsequent iterations. Leadership and development innovators will need to locate partners within and/or outside their organizations willing to join in the collaborative process creating prototypes that push the boundaries of existing practices.

The principles of this matter will revolve on:

- Building more collective, rather than individual, leadership in the network.

- Focus on development vertically, not just horizontally.

- Transfer greater ownership of development back to the people.

Keep in mind that these tactics are not absolute solutions to the matter. Innovative breakthroughs apropos of leadership may come from networks of people who can assemble, disassemble and recombine a variety of ideas and concepts from diverse domains.

While leadership development communities currently exist with this aim, many limit their capacity for innovation by being excessively homogenous, with most of them being from HR-related backgrounds (along with cultural similarities).

This, in turn, limits the effectiveness of these collectives, both in terms of the similarity of the ideas they bring as well as the implementations of those ideas, which may fail to take into account the different values and priorities of stakeholders who will have to engage in any new practices.

In the years to come, innovative leadership development networks will need to increase the number of perspectives that they bring together by crossing outside of the boundaries of the leadership development community and engaging other stakeholders to help come up with transformative innovations.

Conferences that bring leadership development people together may, in time, give way to virtual networks facilitated by Organizational Development practitioners, which connect diverse groups of people who all have a stake in the process: executives, supervisors, customers, suppliers, including leadership development specialists.

Considering how much work and a new form of thinking people will have to develop, this venture will require a different skill set for many research and development specialists who must transfer from creating the programs for the executives to becoming the social facilitators of a construction process that involves all of the stakeholders in the system.

This poses the greatest challenge because it is not easy to manage the network of social connections in order to assemble the maximum number of perspectives and integrate them.

Differences tend to emerge, and arguments follow, yet that doesn't mean we give up. Disagreeing is part of the process of achieving a common goal.

Chapter Eleven - Mentorship

It is no secret that any person who went on to lead his or her people had someone who helped guide them in a variety of disciplines. If you look into the life of any historical figure, they often credit someone who helped them pave the way. These individuals weren't always well-known, but one thing's certain, without their help, the leader would never have been formed in the first place. These individuals are in the class of mentors.

When you hear the word mentor, you would probably recall words like a coach, teacher, guide, pathfinder, leader, advisor, counselor, director, caretaker, and friend.

All of the words tend to reflect certain notions that seem to fit various definitions and ideas around the concept of what a mentor is.

The concept of a mentor goes back to the Greek mythology of Odysseus. When leaving for battle, he asked his female friend, the goddess of wisdom Athena, to take on the male form of Mentor to watch and guide his son Telemachus while he was away. This began the notion of placing the term mentor over those who are placed in the role of guidance and caretaker.

The conceptions of mentors have since continued through the centuries and are a reflection of the many values and morals that are taught to future leaders.

Whenever the word mentor is mentioned, images of supportive people, past or present, come to mind. You might recall a teacher back in school who inspired you to follow a particular direction in life. Today, you may have someone in the office who helps guide you when you are in need.

There may be some differences in people's perceptions regarding the term, as some believe that the term fits a professional setting, while others may imagine mystical powers associated with the term.

The different definitions of mentors reflect the various characteristics that seem to define informal and formal mentoring relationships.

Informal mentoring relationships are psychosocial mentoring relationships, enhancing protégés' self-esteem and building confidence through interpersonal dynamics, emotional bonds, the mutual discovery of common interests, and relationship building.

Formal mentoring relationships, in contrast, are generally organized and sponsored by workplaces or professional organizations; a formal process matches mentors and protégés for the purpose of building careers.

Mentoring relationships have been recognized as contributing to the psychosocial development of individuals. For protégés, involvement in a mentoring relationship has been associated with career enhancements, promotions, higher job satisfaction, and larger incomes. Mentors also benefit from this relationship dynamic.

Although mentors may serve as role models and sponsors, people in these roles often have no emotional bond with the protégé, and their assistance may be purely functional, without an affective component or concern for the protégé's psychosocial development.

Whatever the term, a mentor usually represents the superior characteristics, accomplishments, skills, and virtues to which the protégé aspires.

Leadership: An Incumbent of Faith

The definition of the word 'mentor' is unimportant. What's important is the *character* of the relationship and the *function* it serves. There are a few guiding principles for effective mentoring. In order for mentoring relationships to function well, a healthy psychological climate must be maintained to provide a symbiotic and nurturing experience. Such a climate includes mutual trust, respect, autonomy, care, and appreciation.

Mutual trust and nonjudgmental listening are crucial to moving the protégé's reflections onto a level where meanings are made. The importance of giving the protégé a voice lies in the eventual introduction of conflict, which will promote self-examination and further development of alternative perspectives so that both mentor and protégé see an evolution of perspective and insight.

Motivation is critical throughout the mentoring relationship, as are praising positive growth, modeling appropriate professional conduct, providing a mirror to the extent of the student's self-awareness, and watching for signs that the relationship may be transformative and growth-producing for both partners.

Dr. Moses Haregewoyn

There are two basic mentoring functions: career and psychosocial. Career mentoring involves promotion and visibility, sponsorship, socialization, and coaching; psychosocial mentoring is more general in its role of friendship, affirmation, modeling, counseling, and support.

Both forms of mentoring provide valuable access to power structures and an understanding of culture in the settings or circumstances of import to the protégés.

Mentoring relationships progress through a series of four development phases, including the following:

- Initiation.

- Cultivation.

- Separation.

- Redefinition.

In each of these phases, interaction patterns and interpersonal experiences are shaped by the needs, circumstances, and chemistry of the individuals in the relationship.

The Role of Mentoring in Adult Learning and Development

Mentoring contributes significantly to the psychosocial development of individuals. The interconnectedness and support provided through mentoring can be crucial in negotiating the challenges of discontinued, transitioned, and new roles undertaken in the developmental process.

A new person to a career field or life stage can benefit from the encouragement, counsel, and shared experiences of a more seasoned person who can share perspectives, ask critical questions, and provide opportunities for reflection and growth.

During early adulthood, the most crucial developmental function of a mentor is to facilitate the formulation and realization of a protégé's dream. It can also be instrumental in prompting visions for personal life goals.

During the transition to early adulthood, a mentor might promote broadened and integrative thinking and encourage the protégé's consideration of the societal impact of one's dream. Then, in later adulthood, reappraisal becomes an important developmental dimension wherein mentors can

231

help individuals come to terms with reconsidered dreams, accomplishments, and adjusted life and career roles.

Some benefits of psychosocial mentoring relationships are friendship, emotional support, enhanced self-esteem and confidence, role modeling, as well as possible career advancement. Mentored individuals enjoy higher self-confidence, self-efficacy, and self-assurance. Overall mentoring facilitates communication and interpersonal skills, and identity development.

Due to the support and encouragement, protégés develop an enhanced ability to reflect, learn to examine their cognitive processes, and are more prone to assess their strengths and weaknesses. As confidence and self-assurance develop, protégés may adopt more daring and enterprising attitudes and behaviors.

Mentoring can be especially important to first-generation college students and professionals entering career fields dominated by persons of a different gender or race and working-class individuals pursuing higher education or career advancement.

Women in academics in same-gender mentoring relationships enjoy a special connectedness that may be instrumental in helping negotiate the difficult young adult stages of identity/role confusion and intimacy/isolation, as well as the late adult stages of generativity/stagnation and ego integrity/despair.

In the early adult stage of identity development versus role confusion, a mentor may play a significant role. Through modeling, listening, and encouragement, the mentor can help the protégé develop self-assurance and confidence in their newly developing roles.

Mentoring experiences can also be important in later adulthood, as mentors demonstrate generativity and pursue ego integrity through volunteer work, writing, or continued learning.

The mentoring relationship may also have reciprocal value to the mentor as well, as the experience provides an important source of generativity and stimulates the mentor to higher levels of introspective review. As the author of this book, I have had the privilege of meeting great leaders, including world leaders, and learned from each of those interactions.

However, I want to briefly address the importance of mentorship to my own professional growth and its impact on my leadership. Having come from a religious profession as an ordained minister and with limited business administration at the time, I was mentored by Joe Nocito, the then President of Automated Health Systems.

I am forever grateful for his counsel and coaching, as well as for the opportunity to observe him in his interactions with others personally.

Having to manage thousands of employees under his leadership, Joe demonstrated a genuine involvement and knowledge of those he employed on a personal level.

I observed him as he remembered each of their names, birthdays, tragedies, private communications, their desires for developmental change. Moreover, I tuned into how these principles went to the core of his being because Joe desires personal growth for himself (generativity).

Those who are great at mentoring are always learning from the experience of mentoring and mining for personal growth as well. Joe mentored and polished me for years - personally and professionally - having seen something of my true potential and ability to contribute to the world at large. This ultimately culminated in his asking me to take his place as President after over fifty years of being in that role.

Leadership: An Incumbent of Faith

As a person of faith, I am always motivated to assist and elevate my fellow man. As I now continue to mentor others, I, too, have been influenced to the core as to the importance of enriching the lives of those I identify as future leaders.

Although that was my experience from being mentored, the psychosocial benefits of mentoring relationships may vary significantly depending on the gender of the individuals involved.

For example, the shared experiences, empathy, and potential for deeper emotional bonds between female mentors and protégés may not be enjoyed by male mentor pairings. In these pairings, there will be constant vigilance in maintaining social propriety and avoiding sexual innuendo.

Mentoring in an educational context could be significantly power-laden, especially depending on the gender of the mentor.

Our needs for mentors change as we develop throughout adulthood; our mentors and the nature of the relationship may change as well.

Mentors assume a plethora of roles and functions, sometimes standing behind students in a supportive stance, walking ahead as a guide, engaging students to face to face while listening and questioning, then finally standing shoulder to shoulder.

The developmental benefits of mentoring are significant and promising. Among the most common is the use of mentoring to promote cognitive development and intentional learning.

Transformative Nature of Mentoring Relationships

Mentoring is considered to carry a weighted social responsibility as well as to have a spiritual component, as it has long been recognized in religious traditions and various helping professions.

Mentoring should be reciprocal, supportive, and creative partnerships of equals.

This is important, especially in peer mentoring, where there is less emphasis on role-defined relationships, and both parties take risks with one another beyond their professional roles.

Mentoring can promote transformative learning and development by fostering an examination of underlying assumptions, encouraging reflective engagement between mentor and protégé, providing a deeper understanding of the dynamics of power in relationships, and developing more integrative thinking.

Limitations of Mentoring Relationships

Mentoring is viewed as an altruistic, productive, and even generative activity-good for both mentor and protégé.

However, there are limitations associated with mentoring activities and relationships. Mentoring processes and outcomes are power-laden, frequently unexamined, and uncritically applied. Paradoxically, although women are often left out of formal mentoring programs and might benefit more from informally arranged relationships, there are fewer opportunities for women to be mentored.

This is partially due to the unavailability of individuals willing and capable of serving as mentors and because women are seldom included in the informal settings where mentoring relationships are initiated, such as golf courses, private clubs, or sporting events.

Dr. Moses Haregewoyn

Unfortunately, there remain social taboos and suspicion of close relationships between mentoring partners in cross-gender mentoring relationships.

In addition, there can be difficulties with cross-gender mentoring such as stereotypical assumptions regarding the importance of a career and potential resentment by peers of both members in the mentoring relationship - thus limiting the psychosocial developmental potential in cross-cultural mentoring relationships.

Many mentoring programs pair protégés with administrators or supervisors under the assumption that the senior person is in a natural position to recognize both the abilities and future promise of the mentored individual. This may be not only disadvantageous but also inappropriate.

Although supervisors may be in a position to motivate, they may also function in an evaluative capacity, with potentially punitive functions, regarding the protégé's performance.

Additionally, the administrative relationship may preempt the open, communicative, and trusting climate necessary for effective mentoring. Finally, administrators are frequently isolated from their peers, thus compromising their ability to be empathetic, supportive, and even trusted.

Self-chosen mentoring relationships are the most valuable and productive; there is a tendency for mentors and protégés to choose mentoring partners most like themselves.

This tendency, however, may prevent the sharing of differing perspectives, compromising the full development of the protégé and limiting the learning benefit to the mentor as well.

Mentoring relationships can be difficult. In certain circumstances, they can even be destructive if a battle occurs during a termination during the later mentoring stage, and both mentor and protégé suffer from ambivalence and anger, gratitude, and resentment simultaneously.

Regardless of whether the relationship ends abruptly or slowly, by choice or force, both the mentor and protégé may experience emotions and reactions ranging from rejuvenation to rancor, from abandonment to liberation.

Types of Mentorships

Many researchers agree that mentoring, in general, is beneficial to protégés; informal mentorship may be more beneficial and generally develop naturally and voluntarily between mentors and protégés as a result of a mutual desire to engage in a mentoring relationship.

Individuals with informal mentors tend to receive higher compensation and promotions in an organization than non-mentored and higher compensation than formally mentored employees. Protégés with formal mentors do not tend to gain any career advantages over non-mentored individuals.

Additionally, gender-based differences play a role. Mentorships with male partners receive the most compensation, followed by female protégés with male mentors, male protégés with female mentors, and female protégés with female mentors.

However, comparing informal and formal mentoring without controlling for quality or satisfaction within the mentoring relationship may present a simplistic and erroneous picture. The contentment that mentoring instills on a continuum and the level of satisfaction in the relationship is a key variables in determining the type of mentoring efficacy.

Although informal mentorship may appear to be more prevalent and beneficial to protégés, formal mentoring is an emerging trend.

Formal mentoring programs have existed since the late 1970s and 1980s and have been linked to affirmative action. However, as organizations have become more sensitive to the influx of women and minorities in the workplace within the last decade, there has been considerable growth in such programs.

Despite the growth of formal mentoring programs, some researchers believe that protégés who had input into the matching process viewed their mentorship experience differently than those who did not. In terms of comparing the type of relationship, protégés reported being more satisfied with informal mentors than formal mentors.

This could be due to the fact that formal mentoring programs had limited impacts on attitudes and degree of satisfaction with the mentoring relationship.

Characteristics and Traits

There are certain personal dispositions that distinguish protégés from non-protégés as well as characteristics and personality traits that influence the selection process for protégés and mentors.

Dr. Moses Haregewoyn

Protégés tend to have higher needs for achievements and power than non-protégés. A mentor's intention to mentor is usually linked to a mentor's internal locus of control and upward striving. Managerial employees' motivation to mentor may be predicted by individual characteristics.

These individuals possess traits such as altruism, positive affectivity, situational characteristics that include an organizational reward system emphasizing employee development, and opportunities to interact on the job.

Motivation to mentor may be related to the intangible rewards of the act itself, such as generativity, which requires an element of selflessness.

There are two overall factors that explain why mentors choose to become mentors: other-focused and self-focused. Within these two factors, there are thirteen dimensions. The dimension associated with other focus includes the desire to pass on information to others, to build a competent workforce, to help others, to help others succeed, to help the organization, and to help minorities and women move through the organizational ranks.

For the mentors themselves, the self-focused dimension included gratification at seeing others grow, free time for other pursuits, a personal desire to work with others, increased personal learning, pride, or a desire to have an influence on and respect from others.

From a pragmatic perspective, the research done on characteristics and personality traits suggests specific attributes that may be influential in forming a mentoring relationship, such as open communication, expertise, interests, and expectations within the organization for prospective mentors and protégés.

There are several factors that have been identified that influence a mentor's selection of a protégé. Some mentors considered the protégé a reflection of themselves.

Personality indicators, such as good interpersonal skills, confidence, and dependability, were among those mentors mentioned as influencing the selection process.

When values tend to be similar and shared by mentors and protégés, that can be influential to the dynamic shared between the two.

Moreover, gender also plays a role in the selection process. Same-sex relationships occur more frequently than cross-gender relationships, and the sex of the mentor or protégé is a strong predictor of the sex of the corresponding partner.

Male mentor/female protégé relationships do exist, but as I have outlined, these relationships are infrequent due to perceptions and actual experiences of sexuality and intimacy. Women often fear that the male mentor or others will construe approaching the male mentor or others will construe approaching the male mentor as a sexual advance within the organization.

The actual or perceived power of a male mentor over a female protégé may also create concern about the potential for sexual harassment.

Over and above sexuality, intimacy, or sexual harassment issues, cross-gender relationships are often subject to public scrutiny and suspicion, peer resentment, and the potential lack of appropriate role modeling. Collusion in assuming stereotypical roles is another complexity of cross-gender mentorships.

Cross-race mentorships suffer from public scrutiny, lack of identification and role modeling, and skepticism about intimacy. All of these issues affect the formation of positive, effective mentoring relationships.

Organizations need to pay attention to gender, cross-gender, and cross-race effects on mentoring. Establishing formal mentoring programs may help legitimize cross-gender mentoring relationships by alleviating rumors and speculation that may otherwise occur due to such relationships.

Further, they advocate that all mentors and protégés should receive training about the dangers of sexualizing the mentoring relationship and sexual harassment. In terms of cross-race mentorships, organizations teach mentors and protégés about identifying and surmounting various race-related difficulties. Another important task for mentors in cross-race mentorships is to help the protégé build a large and diverse network of relationships.

Hierarchical, Nonhierarchical, and Alternative Mentoring Relationships

There is some underlying form of a hierarchy that is present in mentorship. This usually applies to supervisors or bosses who serve as mentors to their employees. Mentors perform more career development and psychosocial mentoring functions when they directly supervise the protégé.

Dr. Moses Haregewoyn

Mentor-managers and protégés perceive a difference between traditional managerial/employee relationships and supervisory mentoring because of the degree of commitment, caring, and trust involved in a mentoring relationship. Mentor supervisors are also perceived to communicate more with protégés. Protégés perceive that supervisory mentors provide more mentoring than nonsupervisory mentors do.

These mentoring relationships do, at times, need to be kept in check and under observation because the potential for abuse of power by the supervisor may start to grow.

This could, in turn, result in sexual harassment, denial of promotions, or the instigation of unfavorable work conditions.

Peer mentoring or lateral mentoring has also emerged as an alternative form of mentoring. This dynamic is valuable and appropriate for organizations that are 'flatter and more participative.' The benefits of peer mentoring are support, confidence building, mutual learning, differing perspectives on issues, and the development of friendships.

The main organizational benefit is that peer mentoring offers the opportunity for synergy and cross-fertilization of ideas and experience, the notion that 'two heads are better than one.' Peer mentoring bridges organizational chasms and contributes to teamwork and improved performance.

The observations gained from hierarchical, non-hierarchical, and alternative mentoring relationships suggest that managers, bosses, supervisors, peers, and colleagues can be invaluable mentoring resources. To promote mentoring behaviors, particularly for managers and bosses, the development of subordinates should be incorporated into appraisal systems.

As a role requirement of managers, these should be linked to broader reward systems within the organization. Providing organizational support for employee learning and development is critical. Providing appropriate training for mentors on how to develop and sustain mentoring relationships has also been advocated as a strategy to enhance mentoring programs.

Pros & Cons of Mentoring for Mentors

Most discussions focusing on mentoring tend to focus on its benefits for protégés, but there are outcomes for the mentors themselves. Perceived benefits for mentors are the development of a support network, satisfaction in seeing others grow, job-related benefits that help the mentor to do his/her job or increase his/her knowledge, and increased visibility and recognition within the organization.

Mentors feel good about the notion of passing knowledge and building a competent workforce that represents benefits extending beyond themselves. This brings benefits that include career revitalization, social recognition, and personal satisfaction.

Mentors learn from the mentoring process and experience work-related and personal benefits.

Despite some of the positive benefits that have been linked to mentoring, there are still some negative consequences, including jealousy, over-dependence, and unwanted romantic or sexual involvement. Other problems include the time required for mentoring, perceived favoritism to the protégé, potential abuse of the relationship by the protégé, and feelings of failure.

Communicating the positive benefits of mentoring within organizations may encourage more potential mentors and protégés to seek mentoring within the workplace. Recognizing that such relationships require vigilance to prevent potential abuses is also critical.

Mentoring in Educational Institutions

Mentoring doesn't always have to be within workplaces. They have been present in schools and colleges where teachers have helped guide students on both academic and personal matters. Some mentorship relationships develop naturally without any formal structure or support.

Student & Beginning Teachers

The initial year of teaching is very challenging for beginning teachers, and novice teachers often face isolation. Consequently, many colleges and universities provide student teaching opportunities, and a growing number of educational institutions have implemented mentoring programs to assist new teachers.

When researching this matter, there are four criteria to consider:

- A focus on the roles and responsibilities of those involved in training student teachers.

Dr. Moses Haregewoyn

- An analysis of the stages of development that student teachers experience and corresponding models of mentoring to meet those stages of development.

- The stages of mentoring and interpersonal aspects of learning to teach.

- The notion is that mentors bring their own values and perspectives to the mentoring task.

Student teachers experience different roles and outcomes from their mentors and academic supervisors who partner to provide mentoring to them. The classroom teacher often focuses on craft knowledge, whereas academic supervisors generally provide more teaching process learning theory guidance.

However, questions remain about how student teachers integrate this knowledge and if they learn what is intended through their interactions with classroom teachers and academic supervisors.

Preparing mentors does enable them to be more successful in supporting protégés' success. Specifically, protégés of trained mentors tend to show more evidence of developing and sustaining more workable classroom routines, managing instruction more smoothly, and gaining student cooperation in academic tasks.

The presence of the mentor is not sufficient- the skills and knowledge of the mentor are critical to the relationship. Mentors do not necessarily guarantee those novice teachers will become more skilled at teaching.

Faculty/Staff Mentors & College Students

Cultural observers have noted that plenty of students tend to struggle to establish relations with their faculty members, especially when it comes to the mentoring dynamic. This could be due to increased sensitivity towards legal issues such as sexual harassment, and the ramifications of inappropriate relationships with students may discourage faculty from mentoring graduate students.

Yet, overall, students generally received more psychosocial mentoring functions and were satisfied with their experiences.

Telementoring

With digital technology taking a much more ardent and evident role in our working lives, it cannot be denied that the devices will alter and affect dynamics when it comes to mentorship. The debate regarding these devices tends to circulate around communication, which is easily and quickly altered.

Currently, it is difficult to predict the value of any single innovation; there is little doubt technological advancement affects virtually every aspect of our lives.

These changes are evident in our daily lives. Whether it's the clothes we wear or the car we drive, these are all results of the technological innovation that has been taking place. Automated machines have replaced a large part of the human workforce involved in the mass production of goods and services.

When we place a phone call, what greets us at the other end of the line isn't generally another human being but, rather, an automated voice. The internet's played a considerable role in making the world more accessible and easier to navigate, which has fundamentally changed how we conduct our personal and professional affairs.

Despite the ubiquity of computer technology in the current world, we might reasonably wonder if technology has, in every case, made real improvements in the quality of our lives and relationships.

On a daily basis, we are bombarded with countless advertisements telling us how to have a more fulfilling life through the use of technological innovation.

At home and work, we're routinely barraged with ads for the latest software, the fastest computer, or the highest-speed internet connection, every element geared toward making us more productive. Technology's a rich resource that has substantially enhanced our lives, but it isn't a panacea for problems that occur in human relationships, such as those that can be dealt with in personal, face-to-face mentoring.

Mentoring has always been a fundamentally human, interpersonal, and value-laden concept. When a digital device enters into the mix, it's bound to bring some complexities with it. We know when it comes to the Millennials and Gen-Z, technology is altering the nature of human relationships.

Does the question emerge of how the homogenizing effect of digital technology will affect fundamental and valued differences among human beings?

If digital technologies are uncritically adopted in the face of vital human needs and differences, will important social and individual issues go unacknowledged and, therefore, unresolved? This brings us to the matter of Telementoring.

What is Telementoring?

In order to understand what Telementoring is, a traditional understanding of mentoring is needed. We know it is based on one person teaching another and guiding them on professional and personal matters, but there are some expectations that come with it. Some of these generally remain unspoken such as assuming the mentor will be older in age. Recent formulations regard age as increasingly irrelevant, whereas knowledge, skill, expertise, and experience have become more essential. How that knowledge, skill, and expertise are shared may vary.

There are three models of mentoring:

- The apprenticeship model is in which the protégé observes and learns from the mentor.

- The competency model is in which the mentor gives systematic feedback to protégés about their skills and expertise.

- The reflective model in which mentors support protégés in becoming reflective practitioners.

Other understandings of mentoring identify three broad purposes served by mentoring programs:

- Educational or academic mentoring.

- Career mentoring.

- Personal development mentoring.

With the advent of online applications for teaching and learning, Telementoring has been conceptualized as the online or electronic version of mentoring. Telementoring essentially serves the same purposes as traditional mentoring but uses technology to facilitate mentoring relationships.

Typically, the interaction between mentor and protégé occurs through e-mail, but it may also entail communication via numerous technologies such as instant messaging, audio and video conferencing, and online discussion boards.

As such, Telementoring may occur in both synchronous and asynchronous formats. Other terms for Telementoring include e-mentoring, cyber-mentoring, or virtual mentoring.

Dr. Moses Haregewoyn

Impact of Technology on the Mentoring Relationship

Owing to wider possibilities for interaction between mentor and protégé through the compression of time and location, Telementoring provides advantages over traditional modes of mentoring by linking mentors and protégés who could not otherwise interact.

Interaction between mentors and protégés has become easier since messages can be sent anytime. Due to this, time and geographical location can be reconfigured to suit human needs instead of human interaction being subjected to the limitations of time and distance. Adult educators can more easily link learners with experts across continents and time zones using global digital technologies.

The Essence of Mentoring- Establishing Relationships

We know mentoring centers around establishing a meaningful, deep, and highly personal relationship between mentor and protégé.

Leadership: An Incumbent of Faith

Mentoring involves three crucial dimensions of interpersonal interaction:

- Expressing care and concern.

- Opening oneself.

- Leading incrementally.

Beyond the fairly straightforward exchange of information that occurs in mentoring, mentors and protégés share a highly personal and, ideally, mutually satisfying relationship based on understanding, appreciation, and respect. Issues may emerge when mentoring occurs in online environments.

Since email is frequently used, communication is often limited to the exchange of digital text transmissions.

However, since email and other forms of online communication are asynchronous, text-based, and relatively fast, they are significantly different from face-to-face or even telephone interactions. Protégés attend training sessions to be prepared to communicate appropriately and adequately online with their mentors because email lacks the full range of communication cues that humans rely on in face-to-face interactions.

Dr. Moses Haregewoyn

The use of emojis or ALL CAPITAL LETTERS, or other text-based communication techniques can help to compensate for the absence of voice intonation, body language, and facial expressions typical of in-person conversation. Despite these cues, there is still a risk of misinterpretation or misunderstanding, which can be resolved at some later time by the next email or digital form of communication.

These factors point to the digital environment as having the potential to sacrifice the richness of human communication. Webs of significance that connect humans together in symbolically constituted forms of relationships are difficult to reproduce in digital format.

Other issues involved in creating meaningful mentor relationships concern power and status issues between mentor and protégé. Inattention to the issue of matching protégé to mentor can produce mentoring relationships that are unbalanced, such as where the senior person initiates contact and directs the interaction more frequently than the protégé.

Similarly, protégés who seek advice via email but must wait for several days to receive responses can be left wondering

Leadership: An Incumbent of Faith

if there is truly caring and mutually beneficial mentoring at work. Other technological innovations, such as wireless devices, inherently truncate human interaction so that conversations are reduced to an exchange of quick, short messages.

Aspects of mentoring relationships where sustained communication and psychological and emotional support are important would be sacrificed in favor of quick and immediate communication.

With the wider availability of such wireless services, communication between mentors and protégés could take a sharp technological turn in the coming years.

No longer bound by the need for face-to-face or even telephone conversations, short and instant communication is widely possible and could make a real impact on

Telementoring in the years ahead.

However, unless Telementoring relationships are organized so that technology complements rather than replaces face-to-face communication, the effect of quick and abbreviated communication may not lead to improvements in the structure of mentoring relationships.

Dr. Moses Haregewoyn

Yet, mentoring relationships could be enhanced because mentors and protégés have access to each other in ways not previously possible.

Models of Telementoring

Telementoring is a relatively new concept that has emerged recently. Most of the research done on this matter can be divided into two categories: educational and career-related.

Educational applications of Telementoring typically involve linking students with subject matter experts who provide guidance or information to students in learning environments.

Learning environments can be classroom based, online, or a combination of both.

Career development is a second major category in which Telementoring occurs. It is either a complement to traditional mentoring programs or an innovation that extends mentoring in new directions.

260

Leadership: An Incumbent of Faith

Some Telementoring projects incorporate features of both educational and career-related designs by linking professionals with students currently enrolled in educational institutions to provide subject matter guidance as well as career advice and support.

Telementoring can be divided into three broad categories: pair mentoring, group mentoring, and asking an expert. Pair mentoring involves a long-term relationship between a protégé and a mentor.

In this category, the mentor provides not only information but also social and psychological support for the protégé. Social development is considered as important as the acquisition of knowledge or skill.

Technological resources such as email, audio, video, and other enhanced technologies are frequently used.

In group mentoring, an expert or group of experts are matched with a protégé or a group of protégés. Group mentoring may involve single interaction or sustained series of interactions over a long period of time. Even in this, there is an involvement of basic computer technology, including appropriate software such as chat rooms, bulletin boards, instant messaging, or email.

The 'ask an expert' approach is usually a single or short-term exchange where protégés or novices ask an expert for guidance and assistance. The novices are expected to post questions to mentors, who serve primarily as knowledgeable sources of support and guidance.

Mentors post answers to electronic archives or bulletin boards for later reference or use.

The protégé receives short-term advice, instruction, or guidance from the mentor. The central feature of this model is information sharing between the mentor and protégé.

This formulation of mentoring alters the traditional concept of mentor, where an ongoing relationship is the central facet of the mentor-protégé dyad.

The advantage of this is that students are linked with experts whom they otherwise wouldn't be able to meet. However, this approach does little to promote the socialization or acculturation of protégés that have been identified as vital to mentoring relationships.

Sociocultural & Demographic Factors that Affect Telementoring

Leadership: An Incumbent of Faith

Like many things, Telementoring is also affected by sociocultural factors when it comes to gender and race, which automatically affect the quality and duration of the mentoring relationship.

It has been observed that race or gender tends to multiply the differences in power and status. The personal needs of protégés are often overlooked in cross-gender/cross-racial mentoring relationships. It is critical in successful 'on-the-job' mentoring relationships that protégés have a distinct sense of feeling appreciated by their mentors and that their contribution is as important within the organization.

The needs of African Americans and other racial minorities differ from those of whites in mentoring relationships because they frequently face issues of negative stereotypes, peer resentment, and skepticism about competence. Mentors who take the time to guide new members of the organization in ways that are sensitive to the needs of the individual help ensure successful mentoring relationships.

As a result of the importance of these relationship issues, mentor training is especially important in cross-racial or cross-gender mentoring pairs.

Many Telementoring programs provide only a brief opportunity for exchanges between mentors and protégés, in contrast to a senior person or expert guiding, supporting, or promoting the interests of the protégé.

The brief exchanges between mentees and expert leadership, for example, develop into a 'tele-apprenticeship' type of relationship. The exchanges are longer lasting and involve deeper levels of communication regarding the topic or subject of mutual interest.

Therefore, the purposes and goals of Telementoring programs may vary depending on the format employed and will need to be sufficiently well communicated to both mentor and protégé in order to avoid confusion about what the expectations are for the mentoring process.

Digital Divide: Social Distribution of Technology

There is a general misconception that having access to technology creates something of a rosy picture, whereas the reality is more complex and not necessarily fair. Currently, there is a digital divide wherein access to technology is quite uneven.

Leadership: An Incumbent of Faith

There are people that have easier/more readily available access to the Internet than others, creating an inequitable dynamic.

Unfairness in patterns of access is again a result of mirrored social class, not to mention racial and ethnic disparities found in other aspects of modern life. Lack of access is associated with low education or income levels.

Unless a person has the means to access technology, they are unlikely to participate in Telementoring activities.

Telementoring, Technology, Race, and Gender

Despite the world having made many leaps for the greater good, it remains the ugly reality that race and gender remain a factor in the unequal distribution of access. Be it income, rights, improvement of status, and in this case, technology. In other words, inequitable Internet access remains related to race and ethnicity status.

The mentoring process provides racial or ethnic minorities with vital information and access to the informal network; the process of mentoring minority protégés can be thwarted by inattention to racial, cultural, or gender factors.

As it's been indicated elsewhere in this text, cross-cultural, cross-racial, and cross-gender mentoring sometimes ignites irrational fears and speculation predicated on the existing race and sex taboos. Sex taboos between white males and African American females may produce tension within the mentoring relationship.

Cross-race and cross-gender pairings require care and attention on the part of the mentor and the sponsoring agency or organization in order to minimize the adverse impact on the development of the protégé.

Privacy

Since Telementoring communications happen online, another issue arises which tends to be ignored, and that is regarding privacy. Privacy and confidentiality remain fundamental aspects of any mentoring relationship. With the growing number of warnings about the security of the email, chat rooms, and other forms of online communications, privacy becomes a sensitive issue for Telementoring partners.

This problem becomes even more evident, considering employee communications using employers' computer networks are subject to review by select members of the organization. The reluctance of protégés to probe the issue of organizational problems with mentors via email can dampen enthusiasm for Telementoring as a way to link mentors and protégés across distance and time.

There are technical solutions to help solve this matter, but it requires mentors and protégés need to be skilled in the use of cryptographic software. This, unfortunately, is overlooked, causing a dampening effect on the nature of electronic communications and Telementoring relationships.

Protégés' and mentors' needs and goals should drive the mentoring process, not the uncritically examined promise of technology to solve problems related to distance, access, and human interaction and communication.

With the advance of new technologies such as universal wireless access and communication, telementoring may take many new forms and go in new directions, increasingly opening up possibilities for communication across time and space.

Whatever technological advances hold, meeting basic human needs should be at the center of any development of telementoring in order for telementoring to be a useful and meaningful application in the lives of all parties involved.

Dr. Moses Haregewoyn

Diversity & Power in Mentoring Relationships

Mentoring relationships, in most cases, have been unquestioningly and uncritically accepted as fundamental to fostering learning in the workplace, advancing careers, helping new employees learn workplace culture, and providing developmental and psychological support. It is expected that mentors become interpreters of the environment.

However, there are still harsh realities when it turns to matters of diversity and power. Those who serve as mentors may primarily be members of dominant and or hegemonic groups within organizations or institutions.

Due to this, potential protégés that are seen as the 'other' by virtue of the intersection of gender, race, class, ethnicity, ability, or sexual orientation, may experience difficulty initiating and participating in informal mentoring relationships.

Issues of power and interests within organizations or institutions might hamper the mutual attraction that is required to participate in an informal mentoring relationship.

Leadership: An Incumbent of Faith

If informal mentoring relationships are unavailable to members of historically marginalized groups, then they may have the opportunity to participate in formal mentoring programs organized by work organizations or educational institutions.

Formal mentoring programs were designed and implemented within organizations to provide mentoring opportunities between disparate groups with the combined goals of achieving racial balance among executives and fostering workplace learning.

In addition to promoting workplace learning, mentoring programs may help contribute to increased profits for the sponsoring organization.

Formal mentoring programs have failed to remove barriers to advancement for marginalized groups.

Consequently, formal mentoring programs may not address the individual needs of the protégés but instead reflect the power and interests inherent within organizations.

Mentoring programs may help improve employee performance, but the interests of the organization may be served at the cost of an employee or human interests.

Dr. Moses Haregewoyn

Examples of Mentors and Protégé Relationships

Usually, when we think about mentor and protégé-related dynamics, it's common to assume that there is some professional or rigid nature to it. Some might think that there is little to no bonding involved, but the whole point of having someone mentoring another is to establish a bond. Making a relationship work, regardless of any kind, has to involve honesty, vulnerability, empathy, and a willingness to work together.

This, at times, can lead to clashes and conflicts between the two, but mutual understanding and compromise are necessary to keep the training going.

Both parties must instill trust in one another with the belief that the other is there to help, not harm.

This leads to a dynamic more reflective of our feelings toward our loved ones and friends. A strong sense of companionship can be made, regardless of the different ranges in age and experience.

Just because the protégé is inexperienced doesn't mean the mentor should condescend to them. Instead, it is better to be supportive and motivating, especially when difficult times emerge.

Today, many of the famous people we know credit their mentors for helping them achieve what they've garnered. The myth of the 'self-made man' is now becoming more redundant- waning with time. It's unrealistic to assume that one person fought against the odds and came out on top. Everyone has had a helping hand in some form or another.

The West has been obsessed with the underdog story for a long time, and the reason for this is owed to a long history of the 'commoner' defying authorities to achieve a goal.

The thirteen colonies of America broke away because they didn't want to pay the unjust tax of the British monarchy. The British monarchy itself felt the effects of its weakening authority when it recognized the cause and effect of absolute power on the populace. This makes for an enjoyable story, something Rocky fans would appreciate, but it shouldn't overshadow the other factors.

The thirteen colonies were led by the founding fathers, but keep in mind they each had garnered experience and knowledge earned in their youth that helped pave the way. Alexander Hamilton, who went on to become the first secretary of the treasury, was mentored by George Washington himself.

At the young age of twenty-three, Hamilton was known to be passionate and strongly opinionated. This would lead him to clash with others, especially Thomas Jefferson. Plenty deemed him difficult to work with, but Washington saw that this young, bright (yet slightly conflicted) youth had the potential that makes him a valuable asset. In the early days of the revolutionary war, Hamilton was Washington's right-hand man, helping him form strategies and deal with financial responsibilities.

This is how both men affiliated, and after some time, Washington gave the young man a small army to fight in the field.

Hamilton would not have become the man he did without his great mentor. This applies to many other figures that exist today.

Mentors come in different forms. These include:

- Advisor.

- Coach.

Leadership: An Incumbent of Faith

- Challenger.

- Clarifier.

- Sponsor.

- Connection broker.

- Protector.

- Affirmer.

In the new millennium, there remain people resolutely maintaining these positions to help the new generation find their way in the world. It's worth mentioning that it's not necessary for the mentor to be older than the protégé.

Sometimes both are the same age, or the protégé is, in fact, older than the mentor. The digital age has certainly started changing many dynamics in our world, but the essence of leadership and mentorship remains the same. Let's look at some famous examples where mentor-mentee relationships proved successful.

Steve Jobs & Mark Zuckerberg

Dr. Moses Haregewoyn

Steve Jobs holds the title of one of the world's most famous innovators. From a dropout, he, along with Steve Wozniak, went on to make Apple Inc, a company that ushered the computer into our homes.

Our lives changed in ways that we may not recognize according to man's vision of where technology was headed.

Before his passing in 2011, many were surprised to find out that he mentored a young mind who, too, created one of the world's biggest social networking websites, Mark Zuckerberg. Zuckerberg, like his mentor, was keen on bringing people together from different places. His creation of Facebook utilized the basic idea of a platform to bring old friends together, and he developed it into the world's biggest internet company.

At a young age, Zuckerberg became a billionaire. Facebook expanded beyond the usual social network and has helped create content and establish other businesses across the globe.

Both men admitted their admiration for one another and had each other's respect for what they were both trying to do for the world with their endeavors.

Leadership: An Incumbent of Faith

Jobs gave Zuckerberg advice on how to reconnect with his original mission when things weren't going so well with Facebook in the early days.

In fact, he even shared the places that he had visited, such as a temple in India during the hippy days, to help Zuckerberg remind himself of what he wanted to achieve.

This kind of mentorship is highly notable because the success of both individuals and the companies involved in the partnership revealed great results and ensured the longevity they've maintained to this day.

Warren Buffet & Bill Gates

Buffet and Gates have both admitted that their meeting wasn't out of choice. In fact, both were quite reluctant to spend time with each other.

This was mostly out of the awkward notion that they neither knew what they would talk about. The buffet was an investor, while Gates ran a computer company.

However, when fate brought them together, both hit it off. Buffet would often challenge Gates with questions that made him think differently regarding IBM and Microsoft.

Bill Gates has admitted that he had learned how to manage time and prioritize people as a result of his meetings with Warren Buffet. This mentorship wasn't exclusively concerned with software and business management. It extended into a more philanthropic consideration, and it was Buffet who ignited within Gates a desire to be impactful in larger humanitarian ways.

Gates learned what it's like to be a kind-hearted, analytical businessman and how to begin to deal with larger world problems like poverty and disease.

Gates has gone on to use the same philosophies and transformed this mentorship into a globally recognized partnership with his ventures.

Steven Spielberg & JJ Abrams

Steven Spielberg is deemed one of the greatest filmmakers of all time. His works cross over from films to animation, covering many genres. His work went on to inspire a young and upcoming director, JJ Abrams.

Leadership: An Incumbent of Faith

When Abrams was a young teenage director, he had the opportunity to organize and clean old Spielberg movies. In this process, he inherited a long-time mentor and friend.

Spielberg was impressed by Abram's work ethic and creativity and supported him on his filmmaking journey. They even collaborated on the film Super 8, with the protégé directing and the mentor producing.

Abrams is known to talk candidly about looking to Spielberg for guidance in the past, for help with scripts, film endings, and budgets. This mentorship helped him with his productions and opened up a series of opportunities.

Richard Branson & Sir Freddie Laker

From humble beginnings to billionaires, Richard Branson is deemed the ideal businessman. His charismatic personality, along with eccentric tactics, has made him of the biggest success stories.

Yet, even he was having trouble at the start when trying to get Virgin Atlantic off the ground. In order to find a solution, he sought guidance from airline engineer Sir Freddie Laker. Branson has mentioned that without Laker's help, he would not have made it in the airline industry. For it to work,

Branson needed someone to believe in him and in his idea. He needed to get rid of his ego to succeed in his innovative approach. This is what Laker helped him accomplish.

Considering what they both were trying to achieve, there was a fair share of learning through failure. Branson was very clear in saying that having a good mentor not only shares how to be successful with their mentee but also how to approach failures.

A big part of their mentorship was learning from both their triumphs and defeats.

Oprah Winfrey & Maya Angelou

Oprah Winfrey met her mentor Maya Angelou in the 1970s when she was just in her twenties and starting out in her career.

She credits Angelou as being the greatest mentor she'd ever known. She called Angelou one of the greatest influences in her life. At this point, Winfrey was already a fan of Angelou and connected to her through her award-winning book "I Know Why the Caged Bird Sings."

Leadership: An Incumbent of Faith

Winfrey was looking for a way to grow her business and personal relationships and turned to Angelou for advice on building trust and relationships.

Winfrey said that she always remembers the most solid piece of advice she received from Maya Angelou was that actions speak louder than words and not to take a person on who they say they are, but how they act toward you.

Oprah Winfrey was born into poverty, and through her determination, drive and focus on relationships with great influencers, she became a millionaire by the age of 32. By 2000 her net worth was $800 million. In terms of mentorship, Oprah states that she wouldn't be where she is today without advice and guidance from Maya Angelou.

Simon Sinek & Ron Bruder

Simon Sinek met Ron Bruder professionally, and they got along well. When Sinek had a question, and he thought Bruder could help him, he reached out to him. That's all it took to begin their mentoring relationship.

During the course of their mentorship, Sinek learned that Bruder looked at him as his mentor too. And that their relationship was also more like a friendship or companionship. That mentoring evolves over time and can also be a two-way street. Sinek says, "What I never understood, until I met Ron Bruder, was that mentors learn as much as they teach."

Conclusion

From everything stated so far, we can see where the genuine critical concern lies. The world is changing faster than ever before, and it's difficult for people to keep up. Technological development has skyrocketed at levels beyond imagination. Hundreds and hundreds of years were spent relying on the same tools until the Industrial revolution came along and changed the world technologically, socially, politically, physically, and spiritually.

With the digital age now upon us, our landscape is changing at a historic rate. Not everyone can keep pace, sometimes through no fault of their own.

In a time where we've become so accustomed to comfort and fast-paced routines on the smallest of things, it has led to a generation of youth who are directionless, angry, and confused. This indicates the importance of having strong leaders. The kind of leadership we require in the years to come will be built on harmonizing the complexities of the modern world.

During the early days, it was mostly a one-man show with a set of strong followers, but that arrangement was only ideal for smaller numbers of people. As soon as villages turned into cities and kingdoms, the system to rule *had* to change with the times or fall.

The concept further evolved when nations came into the mix, and currently, it must evolve more so as computers have us interconnected on a massive scale.

This has led many people to slowly turn away from aspects of religion and spirituality. There are more divisions internally among sets of faiths because some people follow it too strictly while others refuse to believe.

When we start to lose sight of our ancestor's wisdom and simplicity, it paves the way for too much complexity and conflict. This is where we are currently. These days, a simple disagreement begins to create arguments, potentially sparking fisticuffs, and the level of tolerance has never been so low.

If we are to progress as a community regardless of where we are, it's imperative to be able to bring people to the table and talk things out.

This is where leaders come in. Unfortunately, in the last many years, we have not been investing enough in creating new forms of leadership adaptive to the changing times. Instances of telementoring in organizations certainly have been picking up, but that system is by no means perfect.

Without the benefit of hearing tone, viewing body language, or judging facial expressions, we have seen how the digital and virtual world creates a gap between leaders and followers.

Human connections are mostly established through interactions and, more importantly, face-to-face interaction. Think about it, would you more likely remember someone who was present physically, giving you a helping hand, or the person who sent a well-intentioned text message?

A bond is established when people are present before us. Prophets made it a point to always display genuine companionship with their followers while delivering their messages.

People from any background could approach these prophets and feel heard. The prophets displayed compassion in the conveyance of their divine messages, and this engendered feelings of being not only enlightened but understood in those masses who felt lost and hurt.

The trait was imitated by well-intentioned leaders, who, despite their high positions, would still take time out to hear their people's pleas. Certain priorities have been sidelined in our current age, where making money and being seen on social media have become more of the driving force for many.

The way of life has become exceedingly more about the self rather than the community. Simon Sinek put it best when he said, "we have large sections of self-help books, but we don't have a single one on helping others."

The streak of selfishness has grown among people, and leaders find themselves in a dilemma on how to go about dealing with team building, given this narcissistic climate.

However, it's too cynical an approach to assume that nothing can be done to fix the matter. As times changes, so do the people with it. It is second nature to assume the worst, but then we forget that although there is a cost to development, there are also benefits.

Leaders will, with time, adapt and make modern-day organizations more suited to the requirements needed while at the same maintaining strong relationships with the employees. Keep in mind when employees see the manager or supervisor making an extra effort, they're bound to do the same, and that's how relationships are strengthened.

This, by extension, leads to a domino effect. Although the dynamics will become more collective in nature, there will always be a need for one person, in particular, to call the shots, whether it is in a time of crisis or because the team believes in that person to guide them when needed.

As clichéd as it may sound, there is always hope. So many prophets came to us to help us believe that the times our ancestors lived in were never easy. Despite positive human strides to make our lives easier and safer, we're drawn instinctually to negative thinking.

It is important for the new generation of leaders to give us hope because times look scary, and no one can be certain about the future.

Millennials and Gen-Z bear a tremendous responsibility in the future, and it's understandable why they're angry and scared. The uncertainty and the growing escalation of troubles across the globe are indeed overwhelming, but throwing in the towel and saying it's not our problem is not ideal.

Dr. Moses Haregewoyn

Sooner or later, the troubles of the world will make their way into our lives, whether we like/want them or not. When that time comes, we all need to be ready.

You will stumble and fall many times, but do not let your defeats become the definition of who you are as a person and what you're capable of. All those who made their way to success did so through trials and tribulations. They had more failures than successes. Learn from the mistakes you make and keep pushing forward. You'll go on to accomplish a lot of what you dream of.

Acknowledgments

There are many people to thank for their vital and generous contributions to my life and the knowledge that has gone into the development of this book. Among those, I wish to express my deepest appreciation is Joe Nocito, who has been an inspiration and support throughout my professional career.

A man of Faith who has never missed a Sunday in worship nor a day in his professional offices, you have reinforced what it means to lead by example, remain open-minded and recognize the hard work of your team – thus, bringing forth the best contributions all can provide.

I am also indebted to the many academic advisors and professors who molded me throughout my academic journey at the many institutions I had the sincere pleasure of attending.

While I wish to name all of them and thank them personally, it would be impossible to remember all of them and the various gifts of knowledge they bestowed upon me.

To my love, Mariam, whose life is dedicated to being the mother every child wishes that they had, and to my daughters, who keep my spirit humble, my mind young and constantly thinking.

To the memory and survivorship of the people of Tigray, Ethiopia, for whom I share lineage and ancestry. It is your undying spirit, strength, and fortitude that I carry within me all of the days of my life.

The endurance the Tigrayan people have shown, even as they have been surrounded by the light of God and their continuing efforts to defend themselves individually as well as their fellow man, has been nothing short of inspirational. I am reminded daily that I can do no less. This book is for you.

To my Cat, Zodu, named for my late Sister and who reminds me that love endures and never really leaves us.

About the Author

A well-respected administrator with proven business and policy development skills - Dr. Moses Haregewoyn holds a number of academic degrees, including a PH.D. in organizational behavior, an MBA, a Master's in Sociology, and a Master's in Public Health.

A man who deeply enjoys human experiences, Moses has traveled the globe extensively and maintained stays in various countries – immersing himself in personal, emotional, leadership, political and cultural experiences of a variety of locales.

As President of a leading national healthcare management organization, Moses leads inspired by this quote:

"Whether your team has the talent to spare or is spare on talent, a leader's goal remains the same; namely, you must bring forth the best from those with whom you work."

– Coach John Wooden.

Dr. Moses does not reserve his skills and abilities only for his profession, as his service and leadership extend outside the workplace. Having served as an ordained priest in the

Dr. Moses Haregewoyn

Orthodox Church, he never abandoned his calling in his heart and deeds, which is why people continue to gravitate toward him to this day. He believes in serving the Lord - whether at work or in the Church. He continues to provide ministry as a volunteer to the community and any open-hearted seekers he encounters.

A well-respected academic, Moses published his research about political refugees in the United States in book form in 2010 with Lambert Academic Publishing.

This work is used as a textbook in the social sciences at a number of universities within the United States and abroad.

In addition, he has traveled and participated on panels at international conferences at the European Headquarters in Brussels, the Chamber of Commerce in New Delhi, Moscow University in Qatar, Dubai, the United Arab Emirates, and New York, among others.

Dr. Moses' faith is intertwined with his business acumen, which he expresses in his academic life and work. A natural born and learned leader in all of these aforementioned areas of life and with a zest to develop and bring forth the best attributes in those he encounters – is the genesis of *"Leadership: An Incumbent of Faith."*

THANK YOU!

www.ingramcontent.com/pod-product-compliance
Lightning Source LLC
Chambersburg PA
CBHW071330210326
41597CB00015B/1402